FOUNDER'S FOOTING

HOUNDSTOOTH PRESS

FOUNDER'S FOOTING

An Entrepreneurial Guide to Leadership and Culture-Sculpture

ISBN 978-1-5445-2716-1 *Paperback*

978-1-5445-2717-8 *Ebook*

FOUNDER'S FOOTING

An ENTREPRENEURIAL GUIDE *to* LEADERSHIP *and* CULTURE-SCULPTURE

CHRIS A. DAGES

CONTENTS

*This book is dedicated to all the entrepreneurs
who gave it a shot. Not everyone who tries succeeds,
but everyone who tries is a success.*

*And also, to my loving and supportive wife, Lindy.
Your belief in me allows me to take the risks
you know so well I'm capable of overcoming;
even when my doubts get the better of me,
your faith never wanes.*

Entrepreneur: a person who organizes and manages any enterprise, especially a business, usually with considerable initiative and risk.

FOREWORD

While the title of this book is *Founder's Footing*, implying that it is, in fact, geared toward entrepreneurs and business founders, the large majority, if not all, of the lessons in this book can be used for personal gain and self-help. I was introduced to a lot of these concepts back when I was a philosophy major in my early twenties and a student of mainly Taoism and existentialism, two of my favorite philosophies/ideologies. I continued to build upon these underlying beliefs and ideologies throughout my college career and experience as an entrepreneur. And while there is strength in numbers and these concepts are meant to be compounded through organizations, I can't stress enough just how valuable and important many of these lessons are for ourselves, in our own lives, every single day. As you read this book, you will see the word *entrepreneur* a lot. It's close to home for me and what I know best.

But don't feel that just because you may not be an entrepreneur or a founder of sorts that this book isn't for you. Because it is. It's for anyone looking to alter and improve their current mindset and create a more powerful world for themselves and everyone around them. So, where you may see *team* or *company*, feel free to insert *self* or *family* instead. When you see *organization*, feel free to replace it with *community*. These lessons can be applied anywhere and everywhere there are people, and they can help us all improve our lives.

INTRODUCTION

Being a founder is hard. Whether you are just starting out as a founder or have been at it for a while but are hitting some rough patches in your journey, you are likely finding that there is a whole lot they didn't teach you in business school. That's because most business courses focus on hard skills. Hard skills are the meat and potatoes of the business, like margins, cash flow, budgets, etc. These are the tools with which you measure your successes or failures.

However, the soft skills are the things most businesspeople struggle with. These are the things you weren't taught in school, like how to be a good leader, motivate your team, create a cohesive and productive team, and get buy-in from your team so they run your business like it is their own. These are things that successful business owners pick up over time, through trial and error. But if you are like many startups, running on a shoestring budget, you might feel like you don't have this time, and you likely don't.

That is why I wrote this book. I am going to fast-forward your learning in many areas so you understand exactly what is going wrong in your business and how you can start to turn it around. In each chapter, I will give you a short lesson, and then I will give you some specific ideas you can use to learn more to start turning things around.

This book is like having a consultant right at your fingertips, though you will be the one diagnosing your business's issues and implementing the strategies on your own to turn things around. Not only will this help you gain a lot of business sense in a relatively short amount of time, but also, you will gain confidence, and you will become a better leader in the process.

I see this book as a life preserver. The information I give you will pull you out of the deep waters of despair you may be drowning in and place you on a firm footing as a founder—the leader your team will follow to achieve the success you have always dreamed of.

PART 1

SETTING THE RULES

BE COACHABLE

FIRST AND FOREMOST, YOU MUST BE WILLING TO LEARN. You must be willing to be coachable and realize, very simply, that you do not know what you do not know—bottom line. We know what we know, and we know what we don't know, but we do not know what we do not know. So, to be a successful founder or entrepreneur, you must be willing to accept some level of coaching or mentorship into your world. Your employees do too. In fact, it's so important that if you have a team member so incredibly egocentric and stubborn that they think they know everything, get rid of them. Give them a chance to open their eyes and mind to possibility, but if they fail to accept their mental limitations, they will be of limited use to your company.

A firsthand example I can give? Me. There were quite a few times in my past where I thought I knew all that I needed. That I had done enough research, tried enough approaches, and had all the right stuff to make things work the way they needed to (or the way I wanted them to). I took sole responsibility and full control of the situation and things went fairly well. But, after time went on and people tried other methods in the same environment, with the same applications, they got better results than I did. I still did well, but I could have done better, and it was my hubris and know-it-all attitude that kept me from optimal performance. Had I listened to my cohorts earlier, my "good enough" results could have been "as good as it gets" results, catapulting me farther ahead better and faster. It took me some time to swallow my pride and accept this, but since I have it has allowed me, and the teams that I work with, to perform much more efficiently with much more cohesiveness and enjoyment.

Can you see yourself in this picture in any way? Are you someone who has a hard time listening to the advice of others or making meaningful changes? If so, know that having a coach or mentor can be incredibly valuable. As an organizational leader, you are essentially overwhelmed from day one. That's regardless of whether you have an education or not, plenty of money in the bank to start your company or not, or partners willing to help you out or not. Regardless of whether this is your first or tenth entrepreneurial endeavor, there is so much to focus on, so many moving parts. Between your product/service development, value proposition, basic bookkeeping and accounting, basic workload management, and most importantly, sales, it's a lot. Mentors can help you eliminate some, but not all, of the uncertainty you will face. The best part is you can easily find mentors or coaches who are willing to help you in nearly any element of your business.

You could have a coach for your basic financial management, a coach for your mindset—to ensure that you're staying positive, optimistic, and not beating yourself up too much, and a coach for sales and networking strategies. You get the point. Having a mentor will allow you to have someone to discuss your business with who is outside of the daily operations of your business. They're essentially (hopefully) a mostly unbiased professional who has been where you are and can help you take the next best steps. Without mentors or coaches, you will find yourself struggling far more than you need to be.

So where can you find a mentor or coach? And most importantly, where will you find one who gives you good and accurate information and doesn't lead you astray? After all, there are many people out there willing to lend you their opinion, but do they know what they're talking about? Maybe. Hopefully. A good way to ensure you have someone worthy of your time is to let society vet them for you. Utilize teachers and professors you can research through online forums or those you may have had in one of your previous classes. Reach out to the SBA (US Small Business Administration) and find someone who has the skills and experience you're looking for and has some reviews you can read to get some peer feedback. Find businesspeople you feel are successful, and reach out to them to ask for some assistance. You can tap into people with many different backgrounds anywhere in the world. You'd be amazed how many people out there are willing to help you in your endeavor and lend you their advice, usually for nothing at all. It's a way of giving back to the system. A type of pay-it-forward approach that not only makes one feel good but also helps someone work through their organizational venture. After all, chances are one day you'll be that person someone asks for help and assistance with their new venture. You'd be surprised at the amount of nostalgia and appreciation you'll get when you're in the position to help others as you once were helped.

Now, let's be clear here. Getting mentoring or coaching from someone else does not mean that you blindly listen to their advice and do as they say. In fact, it's critical that you question them. That you analyze and scrutinize their advice. It's perfectly possible that they may be giving you advice that worked incredibly well for them in the past but is not applicable to your current situation. In this case you must thoroughly appreciate their opinion but also ensure that it fits not only for your industry and business model, but also the time and region where you are launching your business. Cultural differences and technological advancements could exhaust an approach that worked flawlessly a decade ago but is no longer valuable given the framework of your environment. Essentially, you're taking shreds and pieces of advice from many different sources and finding out how to fit them into your business. You may not be able to or want to use some of the pieces, but there will be many locations where the puzzle pieces fit perfectly. This is how you build your mosaic. It's a puzzle game. It's always moving, and it's always in flux, and the two main components are knowledge and action. But without being coachable, and having a team that is coachable, you're doing yourself and your team a great disservice, because you need the knowledge and wisdom of those more experienced to help catapult you ahead of the competition. Let's look at a few ways you can be more coachable.

WAYS TO BE MORE COACHABLE:

- Stop taking things so personally. You aren't expected to know everything, so there is no need to get defensive when someone corrects you. Be open to correction, even if it causes you to feel negatively at first.

- Get a new perspective. Realize that you are valuable enough for someone to want to invest their time into helping you improve yourself. If they didn't think you were worth it, they wouldn't waste their time.

- Look the coach or mentor in the eye. This lets them know you are listening and respect them.

- Don't roll your eyes when they walk away. Make sure you consider what they have to say. You don't have to take it as absolute truth, but it could be. Realize that the mentor is genuinely there to help and is making suggestions as such, not to hurt your feelings.

- Ask questions. Get clarity on what the coach is saying and engage.

Questions for Consideration:

Do you feel you are currently coachable? What are some ways you can become more coachable?

Do you currently have a mentor or a coach? What are some ways one could be helpful to you?

If you think you'd benefit from a coach or mentor, by what date will you hire one?

Lesson 2

BE PRESENT

Quite possibly the most important topic you will read about in this book is right here—being present. You may have heard it called "being mindful" or "mindfulness," but we're going to call it "being present" here, because that creates more of an "in action" concept.

So, what is being present? What does it mean when someone is being present? I like to explain it like this: *being present* means "to deliberately and consciously focus on the conversation you are having (if you are in one), the environment in which you are currently situated, and, most importantly, yourself—your thoughts, your words, your actions, and your emotions." This is my personal definition. Feel free to customize it as you move along.

So, what is the difference between being present and not being present? When you are not present, your emotions can tug and pull you in ways in which you never would have expected.

Being sad can make you say something sympathetic, or do something sympathetic. Being angry may cause you to lash out aggressively and say and/or do something you wouldn't have said or done if you were in a more relaxed and lucid state of mind. Being happy may cause you to burst out in jubilee and act in ways you otherwise wouldn't. You get the point. Your emotions can pull you all over the place. However, for those highly skilled in being present, knee-jerk emotions don't exist. Everything is done deliberately and with forethought.

How is this? How can a person be so independent of their emotions? It's fairly simple actually. Your emotions are a reaction to some type of stimulus, a response to something that occurred in your immediate vicinity. They are part of your animal instinct, if you will. You feel a certain way because of something that happened. Say you see a puppy get hit by a car; that is very sad indeed. You instantly feel bad, sad, and maybe a bit sick to your stomach. But then you see the puppy get up and run away, and they are okay, uninjured. You're happy! The puppy is fine; it was just a momentary scare. In the span of a few seconds, you are tugged from sadness and grief to happiness and jubilee. You wear it on your face, you smile or frown, you cry, whatever you do—all because your emotions are dictating your feelings, words, and actions. They are being manifested due to synapses and impulses in your brain, happening at light speed, usually automatically without you consciously willing them.

Now let's take the same example and slightly adjust it. And this time, instead of seeing a puppy get hit by a car and immediately being like, "Oh no! How sad!" and becoming instantly disturbed, you say, "Hmm, that's unfortunate. Let's see if it's okay." Then you watch and wait, and when the puppy gets up and starts to run off on its own, instead of saying, "Yay! The puppy is fine; now I'm happy," you say, "See, it's good that I didn't allow myself to become upset, because the puppy is okay and there is no cause for concern." What you did there was take the same situation, and instead of getting emotionally jerked from "really sad and upset" to "happy and elated," you just stayed you. You didn't get sad, you didn't get upset, you didn't get happy, you didn't get anything. You just stayed you, observing, being logical, and waiting to understand the situation. Just be you, fully present to your emotions about the situation at hand, in full control of yourself and your demeanor. This may sound like an insignificant concept. But believe me, it has massive implications on your life in every way, shape, and form.

You're an entrepreneur or a business owner of sorts, maybe an organizational leader. You're building your dream; you're doing your best. What does "being present" offer you? What could it possibly alter in your world for the better? Simply, pretty much *everything*. Let's take the example from before and change the puppy into a potential client. You're speaking with the client—a client you really want and feel would be an amazing fit for your product or service. You're giving them your everything, the best pitch yet, and when it's all said and done, they say, "You know what, it sounds great, but it's just not a good fit for me." Immediately you get angry. "What do they mean? Are they stupid? This is a great fit," instantly crosses your mind. You need this account. It's going to give you exactly what you need to move forward with your business. But you don't get the account, and you're pissed. Also, you're not being present; you're just an emotional mess. You immediately say, "Well, you know what, you're a fool. It's so obvious this is a great fit for you, but you're too stupid to see that, aren't you?" Trust, destroyed. They will never do business with you. Not only that, but they're also going to tell their network that you're an emotional child that cannot take rejection without having a hissy fit. Not a good look for your business.

Now let's take that same example, but like the second puppy example, you are present, aware of yourself and your emotions. Same pitch, same response, but instead of the polite "screw you," you stop, catch yourself, and realize that you're about to let your emotions get the best of you and say something you'll probably regret. Instead of the tirade, you say, "I'm not exactly happy to hear that, but I appreciate your honesty. Thank you for your consideration."

You hand them your business card and say, "If you happen to change your mind or have any questions, feel free to reach out whenever you like." Ta-da! Instead of slamming a door in their face and creating a bad reputation for yourself, you handle the rejection in stride, earn some respect, and create a possibility for the future. You never know, you may hear from them in the not-so-distant future, or you've managed to create and maintain enough respect from them that you could reach out in a month or so and politely ask them if they've had a chance to reconsider. This approach will make your life so much easier and build your reputation in a way that people respect you and you respect yourself. It's a winning mindset if there ever was one. But you must stay present to yourself and your thoughts, words, emotions, and actions. You need to be able to essentially look at yourself from the third-person perspective. Imagine watching yourself from outside of yourself and being able to manage your thoughts and emotions as a passive observer. There are many things that we would not do or say if we were watching ourselves do or say certain things at certain times. This is as true in business as it is in personal life.

I want to make it very clear that sometimes it's okay to react by leveraging your emotions. But only when it's a choice. There's a moment between every stimulus/response for humans where you can stop the action/reaction and make a choice to be in that emotion. When you've mastered this skill, "anger" is still a choice, but it's a conscious choice. For example, you're driving down the road and someone rear-ends you. You think, "Okay, what's going on? Someone just damaged my vehicle. I better investigate." So, you pull over to the side of the road, fully lucid and not reactionary at all, just curious and respectful. Then the person takes off on you and speeds away. Now, you follow. You think to yourself, well, that was rude and irresponsible, and you start becoming angry. But you catch yourself, because you're a pro at this, but you consider what's going on, and you say, "Yeah, I'm pissed, and I'm going to act pissed. Not only did this person hit my vehicle and cause damage to it, but they could have hurt me, and now they want to speed away and not claim fault for it." Now of course you don't want to become an angry mess full of rage, but you allow yourself to be angry after thoughtful consideration. You choose your emotions, all of them. This way you are always present to yourself and your environment, and you will make far fewer mistakes, as well as catch more pertinent details that are useful to you.

WAYS TO BE MORE PRESENT:

- Think about the environment you are in. Maybe your home office or your manufacturing facility. Is it of optimal temperature? Is the lighting too dull or too bright? These subtle nuances can make a big difference when not in good balance.

- Eliminate distractions. Stop texting or scrolling on your phone, look away from your computer monitor, or turn off your phone.

- Learn to meditate or do breathing practices. These actions can help you calm your mind and be more aware in the present moment.

Questions for Consideration:

When you look at yourself, what are some examples of times that you have been present? What are some examples of times you have been reactionary and let your emotions take control?

How can becoming more present benefit you and those around you?

How will you become more present, and when will you have this implemented by?

DON'T BE BUSY, BE SCHEDULED

"I'M BUSY" HAS BECOME SO CLICHÉ. SO MANY PEOPLE USE IT as a way to say, "I don't have any time for..." Or it can be said as a way to make it look like you have a lot on your plate. Maybe you want to seem like you are really important and have so much to do, or that you're in high demand and you have a lot of projects to handle. But the thing about the phrase "I'm busy" is that it's essentially a statement of relative confusion and disorganization. Being busy is something that a bee would be. Ever hear the phrase "busy bee" or "busy as a bee"? Well, how do bees look when you watch them work? They are usually in a state of what seems like panic or aggressive action, flying this way and that way, flower to flower, looking for nectar. Or maybe they are building a hive, clamoring over each other to get their work done. Whatever it is they are doing, you can probably see the point. Being busy is a way to blanket state that you have a lot of things going on and you need to bounce around from one task to another feverishly getting things accomplished. It's not necessarily a good way to go about your workday, is it? It doesn't exactly sound structured and organized. It sounds more like you might be running around in a near state of confusion trying to do as many tasks as possible. I don't recommend that approach. It doesn't suit you well, and it will more than likely lead to inefficiency and a lack of focus to get tasks fully accomplished.

The obvious and much better plan of attack is to be *scheduled*. Being scheduled is far more structured and organized. It's a way to tell yourself and everyone else that you have your day and week planned out, written in, and ready to be completed. It's a way to ensure that you have prioritized all of your weekly tasks and have them listed out, so they are not forgotten. It's a way of letting others know that if you are to meet with each other, it is to be done in a manner and fashion that is deliberate, with a certain time frame laid out. Just by setting an allocated time for yourselves to chat you will force yourselves to structure the conversation and ensure that you talk about what is needed most. This is opposed to an open-ended conversation where the parties meet at a certain time and chat for however long. It will help you fit more into your talks and more into your week. It will also help you keep your word. By scheduling things in, you must adhere to that schedule; otherwise, you will risk overlapping your tasks and not have enough time to complete them all.

It will help keep your week in check and show those that you schedule your time with that your time is precious and you have dedicated a set amount just for them.

Now compare being busy with being scheduled. It's easy to see the differences now, isn't it? I know that it may seem like semantics, but it's not. It's a subtle message to yourself and others that you take your time seriously and are not some busy bee flying around crazy-like. When people hear you say, "Sorry, I can't make that; I'm scheduled," versus, "Sorry, I can't make that; I'm busy," it makes the clear distinction that you already have something specific in that time slot. On the other hand, "busy" just means that there is something to do, regardless of what it is, and chances are the person you're speaking with is "low priority" relative to everything else in your world. But really, we're all busy. We all have work to do, food to eat, clothes to wash, and all kinds of stuff to keep us busy, and it's in that subtle nuance that you will own your time.

Don't allow yourself to be busy, ever. You are always scheduled. Even if you are playing with your dog or doing a hobby, you are scheduled. "I am busy" should be a phrase that you immediately throw out of your lexicon and eliminate forever. Also, when you hear other people say it, I want you to think about the person saying it and passively watch how they manage their time. Are they busy most of the time—only to never get anything accomplished? Or, do they actually complete specific and detailed tasks when they are busy?

Also, think if you know of anyone who doesn't use the word busy and instead uses a word like *scheduled*. What type of person are they? Are they high-performance people? Do they get stuff done like a champ? Chances are, if you know anyone who makes this distinction, they are far more efficient than most if not all of the people you know who are always *busy*. Go ahead, keep an ear out for this as you build your business and see if you can spot the "busy people" versus the "scheduled people." If you can, I think you'll be surprised.

So, when do we schedule time to be *scheduled*? A lot of people enjoy doing it in the evening, maybe before bed or sometime after dinner. Sunday nights are great for this, as you can be fully relaxed from the weekend and able to look clearly at your week ahead. This is a good way to take a wide-angle view of your week and start structuring your days, making sure that the most important tasks are written in and that you have time to think of anything else as the week comes along. It can also be great to review your schedule every morning to make sure you have completed yesterday's tasks and you have a close-up view of your day. After all, things change. You can't always keep your schedule (however, I do highly recommend that you do everything in your power to maintain commitments), and you want to be able to make slight adjustments if you need to. An early morning schedule review can help ensure that you are being as efficient as possible. Finally, you're going to want to leave a bit of wiggle room in your schedule.

You probably don't want to be scheduled down to the minute of every day of the week. That can get exhausting. But you do want to make sure that you have a full schedule that has some flexibility. Always, and I mean always, keep your appointments with other people. Never be the one to cancel unless it is undoubtedly out of your control (which it rarely is). If you must, reschedule immediately. This will let the person you are meeting with know that you are a person of your word and you can be taken seriously when you choose to meet with someone. If someone cancels on you, it's fine one time. It happens. But be sure to let them know that it's not ideal for you because you'll have to fit them in somewhere else in your schedule. If they cancel on you twice, you may need to reconsider the value this person is adding to your business and make them less of a priority. They are not good at keeping their word, which could lead to myriad other issues down the road. A third cancellation, and they have to go.

The whole "busy" versus "scheduled" topic covered here may seem somewhat trite at first. But by now it should be easy to see that it can have a major impact on you and how you view and value your time and your commitments. By implementing this very basic yet powerful tool in your arsenal you will be much more punctual, consistent, efficient, and trustworthy. It will also help you keep your sanity while you build your startup.

WAYS TO BE SCHEDULED:

- Find a method for scheduling that works best for you, whether it is on your phone, a desk calendar, or your computer.

- Schedule a time each week to do your scheduling.

- Don't overschedule, but if you do, move things you can't get done to the next day or the next week.

- Add in things you like to do, and be sure to schedule in time to eat and exercise.

Questions for Consideration:

How effectively are you scheduling your days now, and what would change if you started focusing on it more?

How can you most easily and valuably schedule your week?

By when will you have this implemented?

RELEARN HOW TO LISTEN

SOMEWHERE ALONG THE LINE MANY OF US TAUGHT ourselves how *not* to listen. As crazy as that sounds, it's generally true, and most of us do it every day. We do it at home with our families and roommates. We do it at work with our coworkers, customers, and vendors. We do it to ourselves even. We have created ways not to listen that are incredibly cunning, and sometimes so blatant and obvious, yet we don't even see it happening. We speak over people when they are talking. We tend to wander in our minds when we are "listening" to others. We think about what we are going to say when other people are talking, essentially disregarding what they are saying in order to focus on the talking points we want to make. This is also a trend that has increased in the past recent years, as smartphones and the constant inundation of advertisements constantly tug at our ability to focus.[1] To make matters worse, many people would argue that here in the United States we tend to have worse listening skills than most other countries. In many countries around the world, it's common to give conversational counterparts a bit more time to finish their sentences and normally pause for a few seconds after they speak. This is so you know the other person is done talking, you have time to mentally digest what the speaker has said, and then you have time to formulate a response. But how often do you see that happening in the USA? Hardly ever. So often there isn't even a second's delay between one person ending their sentence and the other person talking, and many times people blatantly interrupt each other to make sure they get their point in. So not only are we being inadvertently trained by technology to have a shorter attention span, but we are, as a society, being trained not to listen to each other. Obviously, this has some significant impact on our lives and of course will affect our business as well.

As an entrepreneur/founder, manager, or employee, this is of utmost importance. Getting the most out of your conversations is critical, not to mention ensuring that you are picking up on the correct signals and thoroughly engaging with the other person. After all, what's the point of having a conversation if you don't really understand what it was about? Yet so many of us do this all the time. Now, it's time to stop. It's time to look at what it's like to genuinely listen to someone and have a real and thorough conversation with them. One where you pick up on what they're attempting to say, and you both leave the conversation with nothing left obscure.

Therefore, a challenge to you, should you wish to accept it, is to start listening better. It's that simple, so it seems. But it's actually a bit more challenging than that. You must first choose that your desire to listen is genuine. You must want to care about the person you're talking with and be interested in the topic at hand. If someone is talking to you and you don't wish to be speaking with them, chances are you won't be engaged in the conversation. It's far more likely that you'll be in your own head thinking to yourself about how to get out of the conversation, even more removed than before. Also, the subject matter must be of interest to you. If you hate baseball and someone is speaking to you about baseball, chances are you're thinking about something you find interesting, and it's definitely not baseball. A great way to start honing this skill is by talking to people you want to talk to and talking about things you enjoy. Again, it sounds so simple. But it's not.

Let's look at some examples. Since this book is primarily focused on entrepreneurs and business, let's talk about coworkers. I've seen so many self-absorbed founders listen to their coworkers and make some type of disrespectful remark. Whether it's a condescending "yawn" motion (acting as if they're bored) or taking a few seconds to look at their watch (like they have something better to be doing), there are many ways for people to check out of a conversation. But you can't do this anymore, not if you want to be a good leader. You need to be engaged, especially as a founder with a team to lead. Few things ruin an employee's drive to work hard like a manager or owner who seemingly does not care about what they are saying. I can even give an example from my own account.

While talking to one of my business partners about the need to hire better talent, I was mentioning how a potential employee came from a family that had a good educational background. His father went to Harvard, and the son studied at another Ivy League school; their family had a long history of success. Now, at the time we were a small company of about twelve people, and I was the only one there with any college degrees. Everyone else on the team was essentially a general laborer, with a handful of skilled tradespeople. As I was talking with my business partner about this potential employee and his background in academia (something this company surely needed, as we were stagnant and I was looking to leave it), he gave me one of those yawn hand motions and looked away. I interpreted it as a disrespectful sign of, "I don't care; it's not important to me," or, "So what about his education. It has no value" (a slap in the face to me and my ten years of college education). Here I was, helping this person grow his first business, making very little money and missing out on massive opportunities in other industries, and here he was disrespecting me while I merely tried to find better talent for the company. It enraged me, but I bit my tongue. But if it happened again, it would have been bad for both of us. I didn't appreciate that type of disrespectful treatment; few do.

You see, when you don't care about what your employees are telling you, and even worse disrespect them for trying to help, they check out on you. They stop caring about you, and sometimes, they wish you would fail. So, it's critical that you begin listening to your employees genuinely, even if you really aren't interested in what they have to say. Because in this situation you have an obligation to them. Even if you're "busy." Even if you may not like them. This is your organization, and you need to be engaged. As a leader, you don't have the luxury of ignoring what your employees say to you, unless you want to alienate them.

These are habits and tactics you need to master to get further in life. Train yourself to give people your undivided attention. Train yourself to learn how to phase out your inner thoughts while you listen to others speak. Train yourself not to think about what you want to say next while someone is speaking to you. Give yourself time between sentences to pause and really think about what the other person just said. Then, think about what you will say in return. You'll be amazed at what you can gain from this. Your conversations will have so much more value for everyone involved. You'll get more enjoyment out of your conversations, and the people you are speaking with will notice and appreciate the fact that you genuinely seem to care. This can go an incredibly long way in the business world, especially in a tight-knit startup with only a few people. If you're one of those founders that really doesn't care what your employees have to say to you, you will lose their respect. They will notice it. They will notice that you do not want to have meetings with them, that you only talk to them when you want something from them or have an inquiry about the business. This will breed resentment, and your team will fall away from you.

Genuine listening is critical for entrepreneurs and founders. In conversations with everyone from your potential customers to your vendors, shareholders, and employees, real, thorough listening will allow you to pull as much data from the conversation as possible. It will help build stronger relationships and train you to be more present while you're with the people who are helping you grow your business.

WAYS TO LISTEN BETTER:

- Show that you are listening with your eye contact and gestures.

- Ask questions or make comments to clarify or show you understand what the speaker is saying.

- Put all distractions aside and move to a quieter location if needed.

- Don't immediately judge what is being said. Let the speaker say their full piece before responding with your point of view. Remember, you are trying to listen, so you want them to convey the full message without being cut off.

Questions for Consideration:

In what ways do you currently find yourself not being a genuine listener?

How can you become a better listener?

By when will you have this implemented?

ELIMINATE FALSE MEANING

You may have heard the saying, "There are three truths: your truth, their truth, and the actual truth." This is because much of the time humans have a very difficult time seeing what the "real truth" is, mostly because human beings have quite horrible memories.[2] We falsely recall events differently from how they factually happened. We also sometimes think something happened that didn't, essentially making stuff up inadvertently. And we sometimes grossly exaggerate what did occur, making mountains out of molehills, so to speak.

Why do we do this?

Humans have this tendency to derive meaning from all types of occurrences. We remember something that happened, and then we attach some form of meaning to it. This concept was widely popularized during the existential period and made famous by Jean-Paul Sartre in the twentieth century. Nowadays, there are multiple schools of thought that focus on digging past the meaning and focusing on what happened. Just the facts, and then go from there.

As an organizational leader, you must ensure that you stick to facts and don't attach meaning to anything and everything that happens. Understand what happened and keep the nonfactual storytelling out of the picture. Let's look at an example of this to understand it better.

As I was starting a new company selling nutraceutical products, I had to do a lot of cold sales. Everything from cold-calling store managers to making sales routes where I'd visit as many as forty individual retailers per day (I'd map out my route the previous day and run it the next). I visited hundreds of stores and attempted to contact numerous store managers to offer them a free sample. Follow-up phone calls and follow-up visits were commonplace. Since I was a new company with no name brand recognition, and the industry I was in was highly saturated and rife with competition (like most all entrepreneurial environments), I had to really hustle. Some of the stores I went into didn't even want free samples. Others told me to leave a sample and to call back when the manager was in, only to leave me hanging upon my attempt to follow-up. Not to mention, there were just a ton of "nope, not interested" types of responses. It was hard. I began to think I was a bad salesman, or my product wasn't worthy. But I kept grinding and started gaining accounts. I stuck with my follow-ups. I listened to the concerns of the store managers and did my best to address them. Eventually I started gaining accounts and sales picked up; I was even able to turn a couple "nope, not interested" responses into trial runs that had some success. But had I told myself the story, "I'm no good and this" or "my product sucks," I would have had zero success.

This type of thing happens to many salespeople. The constant rejection of sales is tough, and it can be easy to attach meaning to rejection. But you have to understand that a rejection is just a rejection. It doesn't "mean" anything. Of course, you may need to make some tactical adjustments on your sales pitch or approach, or improve your sales arsenal in some ways. However, hearing "no" doesn't mean there's anything wrong with you as a person, or that your product or service isn't worthy. It is just simply a no for now. It's the same as when you're in the cookie aisle and you choose the chocolate chip cookies over the vanilla cream-filled ones. It's nothing personal. Just felt like chocolate at the moment. And really, there could be many reasons for the "no" that may have nothing to do with you. Just be sure that you don't think "no" means you're "no good" or "your product sucks." Only if you hear those exact phrases out of someone's mouth can you draw that conclusion. Even then, that's still a subjective argument, and it's probably not true.

The key is to be objective when analyzing a situation. You'll find that this is an excellent practice in your life inside and outside of business. Subjectivity and emotion can be quite the shroud for logic and can lead you to a false outcome. Don't ever think that someone thinks a certain way of you unless they say it through either direct language communication or undeniable body posturing and facial expressions.

Many relationships have been destroyed because of something that may be made up or interpreted poorly. For example, Jane and Bill are coworkers in the same organization. They know each other, but not too well. Due to a couple of comments that Jane heard Bill make, Jane thinks that Bill is a racist, despite Bill never actually saying anything racist. He never explicitly stated that or posted anything on social media that makes that undeniably clear. But because Jane thinks this, maybe it makes her resent Bill. Or maybe she tells the other office employees that Bill is a racist, and it creates gossip in the workplace (we'll get to that later), and people start disliking Bill. Then, some employees think this way about Bill so often they add meaning when there simply should not be any. It's a dangerous habit that causes many of us to live in a fantasy world that truly does not exist. It's a world we create in our head, based on false memories and subjective conclusions that make us feel we have to attach some form of meaning to something or someone. But do not do this. Don't think something means something unless you can, without a doubt, prove it or have unequivocal evidence for it. Spoiler alert: this also means you. You don't get to tell yourself that you suck at something or say "I'm no good" because of a few misinterpretations of what truly happened or your emotional state of mind. Yeah, sales rejections suck. A 1 percent conversion rate is not uncommon for many industries. That means out of one hundred people you pitch, only one will say yes. That's a lot of rejection. But understand that "no" doesn't mean you suck at it; rather it means you need to either continue to be diligent or tweak your sales style to better match with your potential customers. Master eliminating false meaning, and you will truly see the world in a new light.

WAYS TO ELIMINATE FALSE MEANING:

- Pay attention to your thoughts. If you start to ruminate on something, meaning you are replaying it in your mind over and over, stop and think of something else. This takes practice, but it is important to keep your mind from being taken over by something negative.

- Think about what is true. Yes, you may not have gotten the sale, but that is the only truth. It does not mean you can't become a better salesperson.

- If someone acts coldly toward you one day when they are usually friendly, don't immediately take it personally. If you don't know for sure they are angry or upset with you, don't assume they are. They may just be having a bad day.

Questions for Consideration:

What are some instances you can think of when you might have attached false meaning that only made the situation worse?

How can you become better at being objective?

By when will you have this implemented?

LET GO OF THE PAST; THERE IS ONLY THE PRESENT

As humans, we tend to bring so much baggage from our past into our present-day lives, from things that may have happened way back when we were children to things that may have happened only a few days ago. But this can be a costly mistake for entrepreneurs, founders, or anyone, for that matter. As a leader of an organization (e.g., a family), you're always creating into the future. You're seeing a market need or want and delivering a product or service that may have never been available before. You're constantly looking at the present-day market and envisioning what's to come. You have to leave the past behind. You must stay present in the current situation, but also let go of things that may have affected you negatively in the past. Whether it was failing on an entrepreneurial endeavor, getting screwed by a business partner, making a huge mistake and having it cost you a lot of money, or whatever it is, you have to move on. Otherwise, you might as well let your past dictate your future. Unfortunately, it happens far more than most people think.

Let's look at Bill and Jane again. Let's say that due to Jane believing that Bill is a racist, without any real evidence to suggest it, Bill hears from a coworker that he heard that Bill was a racist and that Jane was spreading this rumor. Of course, Bill is starting to get angry, because it's now affecting his workplace relationships, but he doesn't want to make a fuss because he has so many other things to focus on. Besides, Bill's other friends in the office know he's not a racist, and he's not going to go on a campaign to raise office awareness to clear his name. He's also not going to speak with Jane about it, for whatever reason (which he should do). But he surely doesn't forget about it happening. Time goes on, and Bill keeps hearing rumors about him being a racist, or maybe he even just gets some weird looks in the office that remind him of this whole incident, whether it's all in his head or not. Over time, he builds more anger toward Jane, he "feels" the rumor about him being "racist," and eventually he starts saying some things that are mean or untrue about Jane to get back at her. It keeps building. Then he sabotages one of her reports to get even and make her look bad. Essentially, he hasn't let go of this incident, and now it's manifesting itself in the present, despite it happening months if not years ago. Is this a good way to handle intra-office relationships? Absolutely not. So then, how should Bill handle this?

First off, because this is a pretty bad allegation against Bill, he should immediately speak with Jane about it and likely should have it be an HR-mediated conversation, because it could get pretty heated. He also wants to relinquish this falsehood and have her clear the lie, so having HR involved could help move this forward. This would probably be the best way to approach this situation: take instant action in an objective fashion while trying to keep out emotion with the intent of getting this whole thing out in the open, hashed out, and buried in the past where it belongs, never to be spoken of again—and with the truth being fully known. This way people can get back to work with no hard feelings and focus on building the organization. This is getting the situation completed and not having it stick in the background of either of their minds, affecting their intra-office behavior. This way, Bill can let go of this incident and leave it in the past and not let it bother him into the future. Then Bill would not be angered by subtle reminders about the gossip that was spread. He wouldn't act any differently to Jane now than he did before she started spreading the rumors, seeing her as just another coworker. He would then truly reconcile the situation, and there would be no difference in how he acted or thought before this whole gossip thing started.

Unfortunately, most people cannot let go that easily. In fact, so many people hold onto stuff like this that it alters and shapes how they act and communicate in the workplace—sometimes in ways that have devastating results. Take a handful of examples, like the Jane and Bill example, and compound them. Let's say Jane is the kind of person who does this quite frequently (spreads potentially untrue gossip), and many people in the office are aware of it, and many of them don't like Jane because of it. But is anyone telling her this? Nope. Why not? Because a lot of times people don't want to "make a scene" or "rock the boat." They let stuff like this slide, and over time, it builds up. After too long, you have a team of employees that can't stand Jane. All the gossip and lies she has spread in the past have created an environment of resentment. People start avoiding her. Jane doesn't get the help she needs to perform her projects properly. People gossip back about her, and there are a bunch of employees holding onto the past about what Jane has said about them. These past occurrences now live in the present, and they shape the workplace, and the workplace begins to suck.

When people let stuff from the past live in their present, it alters their future. And when you're an entrepreneur or a leader building a business into the future you surely do not want past-based issues getting in the way of your future success. In situations like this, you must immediately complete what needs to be completed to leave any negativity in the past.

The very first time Jane spreads gossip she needs to be spoken to. She may not even be aware of what she is doing. There are many instances where people do things that upset others in the office, and they may be *completely* ignorant of it. Therefore, people need to speak up and be honest and make sure the business is being built on a solid foundation and in a healthy environment. After all, you're climbing a mountain of success. You surely don't want a bunch of negativity from the past pulling your team down while you attempt to scale new heights. So, make it a point to clear the past so you can focus on the present. Don't allow for instances like this to occur or fester within your team, yourself, your family, or wherever. You must be grown enough to realize that things have happened to people before, and shapes who they are now. But letting negative occurrences from the past constantly dwell in the back of your mind is a form of self-torture. First, you need to find ways to identify what these past issues are that are holding you back. Then, bring them to light to get them taken care of so they don't inhibit your future growth. Easy to say, hard to do. It takes a lot of inner searching (in yourself and your organization) to identify these issues and then a lot of dedication and strength to get them out in the open to get them resolved. But have no doubt, this is massive for your personal and/or organizational growth. Once you do this, you have a new space to create in, and it will help you leap forward with much more ease and clarity.

WAYS TO LEAVE THE PAST IN THE PAST:

- Start to realize when you are bringing your past baggage into the present. You might become better at this by journaling and analyzing your trigger points and what reactions you have that have nothing to do with the present.

- Make sure you handle relationship problems quickly. By facing them head-on, you have a better chance of repairing the relationship instead of letting it get to a place where it is harder to repair or irreparable.

- If you or your team has a hard time leaving the past in the past, you might employ deeper methods for letting go. You can write an angry letter and throw it away. You can practice loving kindness, where you meditate with love and an open heart on a person, a group of people, or the whole world—wishing them all the best—to help you stop harboring ill will.

Questions for Consideration:

What types of things have you held onto from the past that are limiting you in the present?

What will you do to start leaving the past behind and building into the future anew?

By when will you have this implemented?

IDENTIFY THE CURRENT STATE

YOUR AUTHENTIC TEAM VS. YOUR TEAM NOW

THE CONCEPT OF THE *AUTHENTIC YOU* VERSUS THE *WORLD-shaped you* is another concept derived from existentialism. Essentially, there are two "yous." There is the "you" that is who you truly want to be, the "you" of your hopes and desires—your true self, essentially. Then there's the current "you." The person that's been shaped and molded by your world. The adulterated and artificial you, a by-product of your environment. This you is someone who may have habits and thoughts you do not truly enjoy. For instance, many people drink too much alcohol, yet they say, "I wish I didn't drink so much." That is your inauthentic you being a by-product of some artificially formed habit or influence of your environment. When you are truly authentic to yourself, you act in accordance with your deepest desires, heart, and mind. You eat how you want to eat, you exercise as much as you desire to exercise, you treat people as you want to be treated. It's a way of living in tune with your inner spirit, unaffected by your environment as you've grown up in this world. And the same goes for your organization or business and the team that follows you.

It's important to understand your team's authentic self as well. You must know, thoroughly, what inspires your team members. What do they want to get out of helping you build your dream company? What makes them truly feel valuable and part of something much bigger than themselves? What empowers them to come to work every day and feel like they're not just building someone else's dream in exchange for a paycheck and unfulfillment? As an entrepreneur, you're broadcasting your self-expression to the world, and it's a very selfish thing, that is, unless you include your team members and allow them to express themselves as well. Otherwise, you have a very self-centered approach to building your business, and surely, eventually you will have a bunch of unfulfilled team members and/or business partners that get sick and tired of the company being all about you. Trust me, I've experienced it; it will turn the most loyal teammate against you, and they will be looking for a new job before you realize how selfish you have been. And, by the way, you won't, because all you're thinking about is you.

So how do you do this? How do you not only create your authentic self but also an authentic team that you can combine into a positive culture for the company? Well, it's not that hard, actually. First, start with your bad habits. What things do you truly dislike about yourself? Then, get rid of them. Regardless of how hard it may be, just do it. These bad habits are holding you back, they're holding your teammates back, and they're desperately holding your business back. Then, look at the type of person you want to be and *be* that person. Do you want to be a "health nut" but aren't? Well then, just do it. Defeat your habits with willpower, overcome yourself, and be somebody better. Act in a manner and fashion that truly reflects your inner desires. Take each thing you don't like individually and address it within yourself and start knocking it out. It will take work, and it will take practice and diligence, but it will be worth it. Not only will you reshape yourself, but also you will eventually take this transformational energy to your team. Then, after you've done this within yourself, talk to each one of your teammates individually and let them know the process you're involved in: why you are doing it, how excited you are about it, and how much value they're going to gain by doing this as well. Once everyone has had their opportunity to identify and address their own authentic self, get together as a team to discuss it. Get on the same page. Find commonalities and differences and discover a way to make it all mesh and create an image that reflects the team. Not just you. If you create a company that only reflects your self-expression you're not being a true team leader and great founder or manager. Great leaders help others recognize their dreams. They don't supplant others' dreams to build their own, expecting to get all the goodies from the collective team's hard work. That's not fair; that's selfish, and it will crush your team morale over time.

I know this may sound challenging. It's so easy to say, "Well, identify and then ditch your bad habits," but it is much easier said than done. They're bad habits for a reason; they're there despite you wanting them to be. Later in this book we'll look at neuroplasticity, how to overcome these bad habits and create new ones. It really isn't that tough, though, as long as you have the correct approach. What may be a bit more challenging is getting the rest of your team to follow. But if you have employees that are coachable, are present, know how to listen, and have their self-expression involved in the company-building process, they will be much easier to enroll into your vision.

Now that you have your team on board and ready to define your authentic culture, shedding the past culture created as a by-product of the environment and bad, inauthentic habits, it's time to get to work. This is where it's up to you. You, along with your team, will create your authentic team. You must collectively decide what your team is all about. What drives your employees to work harder? Are you giving ownership to them in a fair and respectable manner? Are you paying them what they desire so they can live the life they want to? Are they getting certain control elements of the company so they have the ability to express themselves and not just focus on your self-expression? You must be willing to give up some power and control so that team members feel like they're not just your pawns. If that's your angle, they will see right through you. And the worst thing is, they might not just be lackluster employees, but they could potentially start sabotaging the company. After all, if your team members feel like they're just there to support you and nothing else, they will eventually quit the team. Maybe not in practice, but in spirit. So be sure that you take the focus off yourself. Otherwise, in the end, it will just be you sitting there with 100 percent of the company ownership and 0 percent support from your team.

This is a business. These people are following your dream. It's imperative that you make them feel as if, somehow, it's their dream too. These team-building exercises are a big deal. They help create trust and a culture that is inclusive, where everyone has skin in the game or is getting what they need. This, in turn, will magnify team morale, and the progress and achievements will be astounding. Otherwise, sit there and call all the shots on your own, micromanage your employees, and make sure they know that this is *your company*. Then, they will simply become temporary employees working for your long-term wealth while they eke out a measly paycheck. Imagine how far that will get you.

WAYS TO CREATE AN AUTHENTIC TEAM:

- Spend quality time with your employees; *get to know them*. Make it mutual, so they get to know you on a personal level, too. When you know your team personally, it is much easier for you to treat them like people, not employees, and they will feel they can open up to you.

- Have an open-door policy. Make people feel like they can come talk to you about anything of concern.

- Set regular times where you get together. Spending time with employees either as a group or individually nurtures your relationship with them.

- Have a goal-setting session. Encourage your people to share their personal goals for the next five years and beyond. Be open to helping them achieve these goals, even if you think it might mean they will leave your company. By creating opportunities for them, you are a lot more likely to keep them around and develop highly competent employees.

Questions for Consideration:

Do you currently have an authentic team? If no, why not?

What steps can you take to create your authentic team?

By when will you have this implemented?

IDENTIFYING YOUR VALUES, BELIEFS, AND MORALS

IN THIS CHAPTER WE TAKE YOUR AUTHENTIC TEAM APPROACH and work on identifying your team's values, beliefs, and morals. This will help craft your authentic team much more easily and help to create your corporate charter, which is essentially a one-page declaration that acts as your divining rod for your corporate mission. Now, keep in mind that only so much can be said in one page. This is not a business plan, which may be needed, but you may craft the business plan with this as the bedrock. This is also not your sales strategy, your operational guidelines, or anything like that. It's simply a document that states, above all else, what your team stands for.

Now, chances are you're not going to want to go into detail about each and every team member's personal morals, values, and beliefs, but you'll definitely want to define them as a team. Of course, there are rules and guidelines from both a legal and objective standpoint that you must follow. Per federal and state law, you cannot discriminate based on a number of factors. You must have a relatively safe place to work, per OSHA standards, and you must obey minimum wage laws and things like that. However, these things are just a base for your operation, regulations you must adhere to. As a leader growing your organization you'll want to have some personalization involved for everything else above and beyond this base of rules and guidelines. This is your company. It's your self-expression, and hopefully your teammates' self-expression as well. Make it stand for something more than just delivering an excellent product or service and following basic rules set by federal and state guidelines.

How do you go about doing this? Thankfully, it's really not that hard. Yes, it will take some time, so you will at least need a day or two minimum, as a team, to discover and understand what your authentic team is and what your company's core values, beliefs, and morals are. Be open to setting a few days aside, as this is a big deal and shapes your collective team mindset. Initially, this may sound like a waste of time. Some founders might think they have so much on their plate in designing the service or product and then having to sell it, that they don't have a day to "take off" to do team exercises like this. I'll tell you right now, if you want a successful company you can't afford *not* to do this. You can't afford to move forward in a company that has no direction, no cohesiveness, no real core guiding principles, and no real belief of this being more than just an attempt to make money creating and selling something. Make it something to be proud of. Make daring, unrealistic promises to each other. Dig in deep and really get to understand who each person is in your company. Make sure you're all on the same page and are here to achieve the same thing. Take the time to craft your vision and your charter. It will be your foundational support when the stress of building a business becomes too much. It's something to fall back on when times are tough, and inspiration to keep you moving forward when you start to shake and fracture as a team—which will probably happen. Every team has issues as they grow. Every company goes through some type of turbulence, always. Not just in the beginning, but in the middle, and in the end, always. So, take the time to understand what your collective values, beliefs, and morals are.

After all, you have allowed these people to come into your organization and help you build your dream. Don't you want to know what they stand for? Don't you think it's wise to understand who these people are you work with almost every single day? Don't you think it's valuable for them to know who you are, what you stand for, and feel that they have a solid part in this game too? Of course you do, as caring about your team is part of being a good leader. If you don't, your business will struggle due to a lack of team cohesiveness, and you'll constantly be shooting from the hip, trying to understand where you're going and who you're going with. You'll have unhappy teammates and probably not even know it. Some of them will be looking for other jobs, some will have checked out fully, just getting a paycheck, and why? Because you're "too busy" to make time to understand what the people you employ are all about. Take the time to learn about and be with your team. Craft your vision and your charter. Discover the collective morals, beliefs, and values early on in your company's adventure. This way everyone knows what everyone else is about, and everyone can feel good that they have a true team, one that is supported by each other, the founder, the charter, and your words and actions. If you choose not to do this it will be at your own peril.

This may sound impossible to some. There are some founders that maybe feel they are superior to everyone else. There are some that are simply very introverted and have a very hard time communicating with others. And there are some that are so incredibly loaded up in their schedule that it's very hard to make the time to do this. Regardless, don't skip it. If you can't be around the entire time to make this happen, have someone help you make this happen. So often you'll hear "meetings are a waste of time" in the business world these days. That may be true in larger corporations that employ hundreds if not thousands of employees, as days can simply drag on due to unnecessary meetings. But chances are you don't have a large-scale corporation—you probably have a small team, probably less than fifty people, maybe only four or five people. Regardless, don't disregard the importance of this. As your business grows, the collective beliefs, morals, and values will compound and be significantly more valuable. Every stakeholder in and around your firm will feel what you are about. Your vendors, your customers, and your competitors will see you setting a strong foundation and coming from a place of integrity and cohesiveness. They'll realize that your team is the real deal, not some one-off flash-in-the-pan startup that comes into the scene and fades away in a matter of months or a few years. This will give you a deeper edge, a stronger connection, and a purpose much more empowering than the traditional startup that simply wants to create a product and sell it. You must discover your own beliefs, morals, and values as well as those of the people you employ. Then, you must go out into the market and deliver your collective morals, beliefs, and values to each and every person your team comes in contact with. Each employee must be a reflection of your charter and mirror the core self-expressions of your team.

WAYS TO IDENTIFY YOUR COLLECTIVE MORALS, BELIEFS, AND VALUES:

- Because there can be such a wide variance in people's personal morals, beliefs, and values, a good way to collect this data is by questionnaire. You can come up with different words or phrases that describe people's personal morals, beliefs, and values and allow them to circle the top five or ten that best describe them, or you can have a list and have people rate each phrase from one to five, with one being they don't identify at all, and five being they highly identify with the value. Then you will need to evaluate the data and compile it in a way that puts the highest-rated morals, values, and beliefs reflected in your company charter.

- If you have a small team, this could be done simply by having people write statements on a whiteboard and combining them. Or each person could throw out their most highly held value, and all can be combined into the corporate charter if the team chooses to embrace them.

Questions for Consideration:

How will you begin to identify the core morals, beliefs, and values of your team?

How can your team become more cohesive through identifying these?

By when will you have this implemented?

VALUES WORK HARDER THAN PAYCHECKS

I'VE SEEN MANY EMPLOYEES OF STARTUPS STAY AT THE company despite getting a measly paycheck with no benefits because they believed in the core values of the company and wanted to be a part of something bigger than themselves. On the other hand, I've seen employees who made healthy six-figure paychecks and had great benefits up and leave companies because they weren't in line with their core values. As a founder of a company or organization, don't ever think that a paycheck is sufficient to keep your top talent. Without a deeper connection to their values, the company is merely a place that pays them money for their time and talents. And while that is a big factor in terms of employment, do you really want employees that just clock in and clock out of work for a paycheck, only to blissfully leave your business and care nothing about it when they're not there? Probably not. If you're a true leader who inspires people to live their full self-expression, then you definitely don't want that.

Most adults spend almost one-third of their lives working, one-third sleeping, and the other one-third living: commuting, shopping, taking care of chores, maybe raising kids, and hopefully finding time to do something they find value and can escape to. With such busy lives, wouldn't it be great if your workplace also doubled as a place of value for them, a place where they can go and not only earn a paycheck but also receive some sense of fulfillment? Think of all the unhappy workers out there, the people who loathe their jobs. They wake up every morning and reluctantly prepare to go to work, to clock in, clock out, and be done with it. It's a grind, no doubt, and it's a rough lifestyle that sucks the joy out of millions of people every day across the globe. Why not change that? You can sculpt the culture of your company and create a place where people enjoy being—a place that breathes life into your team instead of sucking it out of them. Do you understand how much more efficient and driven your team would be if they all enjoyed being at work? Isn't that a great concept? People who get to work early because they want to. People who leave work late and do work on weekends because they are emotionally connected to the cause of the company. They're in love with what the company they work for (and hopefully own a piece of) stands for and get excited when they arrive at work in the morning. As we spend more and more time working, why not make work a place of team fulfillment versus a place where all the employees work for a paycheck only to build the dreams of the founder?

How is this done? What if you own a manufacturing company that makes random durable goods? What if you start an accounting firm and are slammed crunching numbers all day and don't see the angle to make "accounting" a business that makes people fulfilled? Thankfully, there are several ways to add value for the team and all stakeholders, regardless of what industry you're in. I believe the best way is through the *for-benefit corporation model.* It's a tried-and-true process that has a global framework of members and guidelines that can help you craft a company that is truly more than a money-making endeavor.

The for-benefit corporation model (or B Corp) is growing very quickly across the world, and for good reason. Just to get clear out of the gate, there are essentially two different types of B Corporations: the filing status and the B Corp certification from B Lab, the firm that originally created the B Corp concept. The filing status type is essentially like a C Corp or an S Corp filing status and is a method for determining a core cause behind the firm's creation. If you file as a B Corp for incorporation in a state, you're saying, "We stand for a certain cause and will grow this business with this cause in the forefront of our minds." It's a noble avenue and a way to take the extra step to tie your business to something more than the value proposition of your good or service. But it is much less regulated than the B Corp certification from B Lab.

The B Lab B Corp certification goes through several checks and balances to ensure you are hitting a minimum number of elements to qualify as a true for-benefit corporation. Some of these categories include ensuring there is some ownership set aside for the employees of the organization, ensuring inclusiveness and diversity in your organization, ensuring that your organization is environmentally responsible, and things of that nature. It's a great way to take a holistic approach and to ensure you are considering all stakeholders of your organization and not just the shareholders.

As you begin to form your corporation, give the B Corporation a look, regardless of whether it's the B Lab certification or the for-benefit filing status (if your state offers one). It will help ensure that you keep a strong cause in mind while you form and build your organization. It will also help your customers understand that you are here to do more than just make money. You're here to add value for all stakeholders and make sure that you have an amazingly strong foundation to build from—that you want to leave this world, and your employees, in a far better position than when you first arrived. If you do that, not only will you be rewarded financially, but you will also be admired and respected for being a true leader, which, many will say, goes a whole lot further than money.

CREATING A COMPANY WITH VALUES PEOPLE LOVE:

- Think about what is most important to you. As the leader of the company, you need to know what you value and why you are doing what you do.

When you have a *why* for your business, you will lead with passion, and this will carry over into your team's passion.

- By creating a company with core values that people can get behind, you will attract individuals with ideals similar to yours, which will create a more cohesive workplace with people all working toward a common goal.

- You might also consider asking teammates what their values are and incorporating them into your company's values. You might set aside a certain amount and give it to a charity in a team member's name or do other similar things to let employees know your company values what they value, and in turn, values them as employees.

Questions for Consideration:

In what ways is your organization currently creating strong values?

In what ways could you do better at creating strong values?

By when will you have this implemented?

YOUR TEAM'S PREDICTABLE FUTURE VS. A FUTURE YOU SCULPT

SO FAR IN THIS BOOK WE'VE TALKED ABOUT DIFFERENT WAYS of being—being coachable, being present, being a genuine listener, detaching your present day's actions from the past, and so forth. These are ways of acting, in the present, that will alter your future if you haven't been doing them already. However, if you're like most people, which you likely are, you haven't been doing these things so well. You haven't been present in your conversations, you may not have been looking for a professional coach to help guide you, you may have been stuck in your past. But now you're changing that, and you're an entrepreneur, and you want your company to have this amazing new approach as well.

You've now spent all this amazing time building your team and discovering who they are and what they stand for. You know what your collective morals, beliefs, and values are; you have crafted an amazing corporate charter and vision; and everyone is staying present in their conversations and you're feeling great about everything. You may have even gone as far as to register or file as a B Corp, anchoring your company's cause to a third-party entity that can help keep you accountable for your firm's actions. But here we are, in the present, and it's easy to realize that your team is on this very predictable path. Without a doubt, the current path looks much better now than before, assuming you've been implementing what's in this book. But it could be improved, and what does it take to maintain it all?

This is where we take the time to look at where you are now and where you would like to go. Essentially, we'll be taking a look at where you think you'll be in one year, five years, and ten years given the current team/situation, and what it would take to alter that path into one that you find more beneficial and valuable for yourself and all of the stakeholders involved.

We all have our habits, patterns, and routines that have been engrained into our psyche (we'll go into this more later), and a corporation or team is no different. After all, it's made up of people, each with their own habits and patterns. Essentially, a business is a collection of people, so it makes sense that your company has its own habits and patterns too. So, we'll be taking everything we have done up to this point and future-proofing it. You will sculpt your company's future through your words and declarations and create anchors in your future that you will be pulled to.

Let's say you've never read this book. Let's say that you've never taken any leadership initiative and attempted to truly build your team. No self-expression, no core values—just you being you as you are now, and your team being your team as they are now, selling whatever product or service it is that you sell. It would be fairly easy to predict how the company would move into the future. If you have a team that is disorganized and lazy now, in two years you'll have a team that is disorganized and lazy. If you have a top-tier sales team that constantly pushes new boundaries and is relentless in their pursuit, chances are in five years you'll have a very profitable company that is run by an incredible sales team. Without something altering or rerouting you from your predictable course, chances are your company will follow said predictable path. It's a fairly simple concept to comprehend. People generally do what they've always done and will continue to do so until they die, as will your company. Unless you, someone, or something interjects and attempts to transform you or your company. But now with all your added tools and your newfound tactics you can craft a future that becomes a reality. We do this by means of making agreements and declarations to each other and sticking to them—no matter what.

HOW TO SCULPT YOUR COMPANY'S FUTURE:

- Sit down as a team and talk about the current state of your company. Visualize what practices and habits are happening now, categorize them into "good" and "bad" groups, and figure out which ones to keep and which ones to ditch to enhance your team.

- Actions that are "bad" need to be removed. By now, you can clearly see that by continuing to do this "bad" habit as a team, it will take you down a less desirable path in the future.

- Actions that are "good" should be kept and built upon. You should also add practices that will enhance and build upon the good momentum you currently have going, to help your business reach its ultimate destination.

- Take the time to alter and tweak what practices you have now. Do this in a manner that gives you a very favorable and positive outcome for the future of your organization. Write them down and talk about how much better things will be in the company if something is altered or some of the habits are thrown out the window. Also, really have the team visualize what this new path could look like if you made all these adjustments.

- Once you've taken the time to get a clear picture of this new potential path, make agreements and declarations for each team member, so they know what they are responsible for. Then, you all must keep these promises to each other to create this amazing new future.

Questions for Consideration:

What is the current path your business is on, and is it headed in the right direction?

How will you work with your team to create a new and better prescribed path?

By when will you have this implemented?

PART 3

KEY CONCEPTS TO EMBRACE

YOUR WORD AS YOUR CURRENCY

IN OUR MODERN CULTURE WE CONSISTENTLY FAIL TO REALIZE how often we fail ourselves. We make promises to ourselves and others that we continually fail to keep. We may tell ourselves, "I'm only having one drink tonight," and then have three. Or "I'm starting to exercise this next week, four times a week and no less," and then we work out twice and forget about it. It happens all the time, in every city and almost every household. Has somebody ever said to you, "I'll be there in fifteen minutes," and then you find yourself waiting for them twenty-five minutes later? There are a million examples of ways we break our word to ourselves and those around us, and surely some that you can think of that you do regularly and consistently. This is such an incredibly bad habit. The worst part is that very few people recognize they're doing this and how much of an impact it has on their life. Let's take a previous example and dig in a little more so we can see how it affects our lives.

Many of us drink alcohol. Some do it very seldomly, and others do it far too much, and then there's everyone in between. For the ones that feel that they may drink a bit more than they should, you'll often hear them say, "I'm only having one or two drinks, and that's it," but then you see them the next day, and they were out until 2:00 a.m. and are obviously hungover from having way more than "just two drinks." But, so what? Who cares, right? Well, you care. Deeply. You just don't know it. Think of it this way—have you ever made a promise to someone and then broken it? Did you make another promise to that person and then break it again? Some of us have. How did that affect the relationship between you and that person? Surely, the next time you promised them something they probably took it with a grain of salt. Because twice already you promised them something and then they realized that your word had no strength to it. It wasn't connected to anything of value. It was simply an empty promise that you gave to them that had no meaning. No follow-through, no integrity. They basically see your word as worthless and cannot trust you. That's not a great place to be, especially as an entrepreneur, leader, or founder of an organization.

Now, back to you. Those times when you told yourself, "just one drink" and ended up having five, those are broken promises to yourself also. What happens after you do that many times over many months or years? Well, you have no power of your word over yourself. In fact, the alcohol has power over you. It controls you; it makes you break promises to yourself all the time. It gets to a point where you simply stop trying to control your urges and drink to your heart's content. Or, you foolishly keep trying to suppress your urges, only to consistently break promises to yourself and get weaker and weaker by the day.

Now, let's look at the flip side of this.

Let's say you go out with friends and say, "I'm only having two drinks, max." Then you go out, you have your two drinks, and you switch to water or something else non-alcoholic for the night and that's that. You wake up feeling good and kept your word to yourself. Excellent job, well done. Now if you keep repeating this pattern and maintain personal integrity, before you know it, keeping your word to yourself is almost automatic. You say, "Only one drink," and that's it, only one drink. Then you might say, "I'm going to run three miles after work today," and no matter how you feel, you run those three miles after work, without hesitation, despite being tired and hungry. Continual positive reinforcement to yourself with respect to keeping your word to yourself can have an amazing impact. Before you know it, your word is as good as gold. If you tell your customer, vendor, or employee, "I'll have it done by Tuesday at 5:00 p.m.," they'll know they can count on you, without question, and you'll have it done by then. As John F. Kennedy once said, "I'd rather be accused of breaking precedents than breaking promises." That's because JFK knew the value of personal integrity. He understood very clearly that a person who constantly keeps their word to themselves and others can be trusted, is respected, and is the real deal. It's a truly monumental way to live.

I grew up in Southern California in the 1980s and 1990s. Everything was so laid-back. Everyone was so cool. Almost too cool. It was an everyday occurrence where someone would say, "Be there at 5:00 p.m.," and then you'd wait until 5:30 p.m. for them to show up. It was contagious, and everyone did it. You could plan on someone being late or not keeping their word far more times than you could rely on them to be honest and keep their word. It creates an environment of, "I do what I want," or, "Yeah, I tried, but I'm just so busy," or whatever. The bottom line is that it can be hard to trust people when this is the case. When everyone seems so engulfed in their own world and influenced by the circumstances around them that they can't control something as simple and trite as being on time, it creates an energy of distrust.

Why is it so hard? Surely one could say, "Traffic was horrible," but you know it's going to be horrible; it's the Los Angeles Basin. I never could figure out why people were always habitually late when I was growing up. I still don't have an exact answer, but I know that part of it has to do with some people thinking they're more important than others and also some people that simply cannot keep their word to themselves, let alone anyone else. And it's a pretty sad reality when you think about it. People who can't be on time, who can't be trusted to do what they say, who are more at the whim of the world around them than their own word. I've heard before that this entire existence we have, humanity, Earth, the Universe, et cetera, is merely a reflection of the vibrations that came from God when "he" spoke.[3] Whether this is true or not remains to be verified. But the point remains the same: our words can have massive power, power that can reshape the world and what we call reality. As the world-famous martial artist Bruce Lee once said, "Don't speak negatively about yourself, even as a joke. Your body doesn't know the difference...change the way you speak about yourself and you can change your life."

We can choose to empower ourselves and keep our word at all costs or become weak and break our promises to ourselves and others constantly, leaving us impotent and shameful and a slave to our habits and weaknesses. It really is that big of a deal. I go through all this because this is how we create a stronger bond for ourselves and our team. We build a strong word, and then we make promises to each other, and keep them.

The Declaration of Independence is such an incredibly strong and powerful document. It was the basis for the creation of one of the strongest empires to ever exist on Earth. It is a declaration that was made by men and carried on through generation by generation to stand the test of time. This wasn't just, "Sure, yeah, we'll see if we can make this happen." This was, "Yes, by all means necessary, this is our future, and we'll die fighting to make this a reality." Many did die fighting, and their cause lives on. A declaration made by a person that has ownership of their word and has consistently proven themselves true to themselves is as good as gold. It's a guarantee. Once you master this, you can unlock doors to the universe you never thought possible.

This is the mindset you must have when you create a new path for your team, when you ditch your prescribed path and create a new and powerful path that you literally sculpt with your words. But for this to work well enough and long enough for your team, you must realize the importance of this concept and understand that the more your team keeps their word to themselves and each other, the stronger it becomes and the more likely it will continue to happen as time goes on. This is what will alter the path of your organization for years. It will take you to the destination where you want to go—where you intend to go. And when you start seeing yourself or the team veer off the intended path, you'll be able to identify where and why, and you'll have the tools to get back on track. The tools are founded on your words. Those invisible, auditory thoughts that you (hopefully) choose to speak. Do not let this concept escape you. It is massively powerful.

WAYS TO START KEEPING YOUR WORD:

- If you currently feel that you are not very good at keeping your word in all aspects, figure out in which ways you could do better. First and foremost, do you keep your word to yourself? Then, do you keep your word to your family and those closest to you? Do you keep your word around time commitments? Do you keep your word around things you say you will do? If any of these areas is lacking, realize which area you have a hard time keeping your word in and work harder to do so.

- Some people find it beneficial to have an accountability partner. When you make someone a promise, write it down and tell your accountability partner what you are supposed to do. Set a date that you will do it by. If you don't, your accountability partner should call you out on it, and then you should make good on your promise right away. Not only will this help you do what you say, but it will also help you not say things you know you won't do. This will strengthen your integrity among your team.

- If you don't want to have an accountability partner, hold yourself accountable. Give yourself small rewards for doing what you said you'd do. This will make you more likely to keep your word in the future.

Questions for Consideration:

What are some instances where you have not kept your word? Are there ways you can fix that now?

How can you create personal integrity and strengthen the value of your word?

By when will you have this implemented?

ACCOUNTABILITY VS. RESPONSIBILITY

ONCE YOU UNDERSTAND AND HAVE MASTERED THE IMMENSE power of your word, you must understand a basic distinction—the difference between accountability and responsibility. On the surface, they may seem similar, if not identical, but they are not.

Accountability, "to be accountable," means that you are the sole person that is to be held to ensuring something is done or is overseen. You are the person "accountable" for making sure there are ninety-nine guests at the party, no more, no less. There is no shared blame, unless it is explicitly stated that multiple people are held accountable for something. But generally, when you are left accountable for something, at the end of the day, you make it happen. You have the ultimate authority in the say of what does and does not happen to achieve the desired state of your endeavor.

Being responsible for something is a bit different. We are all responsible for the health and well-being of the planet. We have a duty to recycle, to be good caretakers of our Mother Earth. But none of us are solely held accountable for the earth. The powers that be can't say, "Mr. John Smith, you're to blame for the poor shape of the earth; you are accountable." It's not possible. The health and well-being of the earth is out of any of our hands. If man-made global warming occurs at a rate and scale that is unprecedented, and catastrophic damage happens around the earth due to it, no one person can be held accountable. But we can all be responsible to some extent. We can be conscientious people and act in a way that keeps our planet in the forefront of many of our decisions and help mitigate the risks.

Without a doubt, responsibility and accountability are different. If you're responsible for something, you have a duty to have something's best interest in mind, but ultimately it is beyond your power and abilities to control it completely. To be accountable for something means that you are the sole individual who is given the authority for the outcome of something, and you do have complete power over it, and it is your duty to see it evolve as desired.

You are both *accountable* and *responsible* to your company. On one hand, you are solely accountable for everything that happens in your startup, top to bottom and side to side. You have full control and have the last word when it comes to anything and everything in your company. Also, you are responsible for your company. It is your job to look after and take care of it in every way. But chances are, others will also be responsible—maybe the owner of the building you rent, your partner who has vested interest in the company, or the trash man that takes out the trash. They, too, are responsible in some way for the business to do well and operate normally. Each person has some level of responsibility, whether they know it or not. In a way, they are all service stakeholders, upstream stakeholders that are directly or indirectly responsible for the functioning of the business. But they are not accountable. If the trash person gets sick and can't make it to work and your trash doesn't get picked up on the Tuesday that it normally does, are they accountable for your trash? No, you are. You always are. Because it's your trash, and it's your company, and if you want a well-run business then you must take ultimate accountability for everything and anything that is involved in it. If the trash person fails to show up to take your trash out, and it needs to be taken out, you get off your butt and go dispose of it somewhere—not because it's your accountability, but because it's your responsibility. You take control. As an entrepreneur/founder, you have to be able to differentiate your accountabilities from your responsibilities, and you need to be able to do it for your coworkers and yourself. A big part of making this successful is keeping your word.

When you spend time with your team and set up team events that are designed to build your company and each of your self-expressions, then you'll begin to start seeing what everyone is capable of. You'll see their desire to want to keep their word and be involved in a big awesome undertaking. You'll see people begin to start making amazing declarations and desire to help do whatever it takes to build the team. And in doing so, you'll need to make sure your team has their responsibilities and accountabilities understood and tasked out. It may seem trite, something akin to "divvying up chores" as kids, but it will help your team remain cohesive and give everyone some semblance of ownership, beyond, hopefully, owning a piece of the business itself. It helps create clear goals and boundaries for everyone to follow, and each of you knows that it will be taken care of because you all have given your word. You have declared in front of the team that you are accountable for your tasks, and each of you has declared that you are all responsible for the success of the company. This is a major step in creating a clear and cohesive yet directionalized team that is all on the same page. As you brainstorm and collaborate all the tasks, responsibilities, and accountabilities for the team, you begin to see people disclose their likes and dislikes, and their personality traits. You'll see what types of responsibilities they are willing to take on and what they desire to be accountable for. You may not be able to cover everyone on the team, but you'll get a good feel. And the one thing that is going to keep everyone anchored to their promise is their word.

It's important that you let your employees and business partners know, should you have any, that your word is your bond. It is your human cash that has value (or not) due to your actions and ability to make it worth something. You built your company on your word, to do whatever it is you set out for, but now you must ascribe your word to a cause and help other people help you build your company and ascribe their word to something too.

Be sure your team members know that your word is the most valuable thing you have, and you will treat their word as such. If someone in your company promises accountability for something and then two weeks later stops performing the task, then you know they cannot be trusted or are not reliable. The same goes for you. You must set a bar so high for yourself that your word is your future and your accountabilities are set in stone. There can be no lack of commitment or uncertainty about whether you will achieve what you said. Obviously, it's important that you set realistic boundaries. And, keep in mind that what you say you are accountable and responsible for are within your ability to achieve, so you don't constantly fall short. But you must also set goals that challenge you. More on that later. The main takeaway is that you set and understand the responsibilities and what people will be accountable for, so you know what is needed to make your business function.

There are so many moving parts in entrepreneurship and building businesses. It's critical that you take the time to sit down as a team and understand what needs to be taken into account. It may take an entire day, maybe more, to do this, but the savings and discovery you will gain in the upcoming year will be paid out in spades. You'll be able to see which employees have integrity, which ones stand true to their word, and which ones are the fastest to slack off and stray from their commitment. Most importantly, you will learn how you enforce your word to yourself and how accurately you can deliver on your promises. Of course, you want 100 percent fulfillment on your word. But that's not realistic. Even 90 percent would be phenomenal. After all, if you're hitting 100 percent of your goals you must not be pushing yourself too hard. And to be quite frank, your company will suffer if you just want to save face and push weak goals to maintain a high success rate versus sticking your neck out to accomplish something amazing that you may fail at. Like I always told myself when I was pushing myself to become a better snowboarder, "If you're not falling, you're not pushing yourself hard enough." The same goes for business. You must hold yourself and your team accountable to a word that is challenging, one that may not be accomplished, but also one where each and every one on your team is fulfilled by its undertaking.

HOW TO MAKE SURE YOUR TEAM IS RESPONSIBLE AND ACCOUNTABLE:

- Make the time for a team accountability/responsibility day. Create a big chart including everything that needs to be done in the company on a daily, weekly, monthly, and yearly basis.

- Once you know what needs to get done, break it down into specific tasks that need to be completed.

- Delegate these tasks to the appropriate team members, and set goals with them for when these tasks should be completed.

- Have them report to you when each task is done, so you can keep track of who is doing what they are supposed to. This will help you understand how team members act, which will be invaluable knowledge for you in the future.

- Modify this as needed. You might do this weekly, monthly, or just for specific projects.

Questions for Consideration:

Major obstacles to setting and maintaining responsibilities/accountabilities:

How can you most easily and valuably create realistic accountabilities and responsibilities?

By when will you have this implemented?

ANXIETY OF FAILURE

Failing sucks. There is no doubt it hurts, and some people tend to avoid it at all costs. Failure, at the least, bruises our ego and damages our self-confidence. It can beat someone down to the point where they never try a thing again. Or, it can cost so much money that many people simply can't afford to continue their entrepreneurial pursuits. It can be so damaging that many people fail once, maybe twice, trying something, and they quit and never look back. But that's surely not everyone. For some people failure is a natural by-product of growth, a learning opportunity and a chance to create new strategies and move ahead into the future with newfound knowledge. It's a necessary step in the business-building process, and one that you must embrace.

Entrepreneurship is riddled with failure. In fact, I'd argue that for first-time entrepreneurs, you fail 95 percent of the time and succeed 5 percent of the time. It's kind of like learning to golf; at first, most of your attempts are not good at all, with some being downright horrible, but the few that are good are what keep you coming back. It's that handful of good shots that gives you confidence that you can and will eventually succeed. And it's the small wins that keep an entrepreneur positive and upbeat, that keep them willing to risk so much with no guarantee of success. After all, most entrepreneurs decide to take the leap of being a startup founder because they have big aspirations. They want to become millionaires or make some great contribution to society. Then, the gravity of the situation hits hard; you realize it's going to be a long and difficult journey and you may not reach your destination. Then, it's the little wins that count. To make the most of those little wins and all the failures you go through, it's imperative to squeeze as much wisdom and learning as possible from all your failures.

Many people don't even attempt to start their own business simply because they're afraid of failing. They don't want to start out on an endeavor and tell all their friends and family about it and have everyone watch them fail. When approached improperly, it can lead someone to believe that they may be no good, or this might not be for them. But in reality, that's how it goes for most people. Most people start companies and stumble and trip all over themselves for years. Only a handful of people nail it right out of the gate, and even they have a period of challenge and failures. No one can escape it. Go ask a dozen successful entrepreneurs how many times they've failed at something and I'm willing to bet that they will all say, "too many to count."

Failure is just embedded in innovation.

When trying something new, maybe stuff that no one else has tried and surely you haven't tried, there's going to be a steep learning curve to the process. You'll have to improvise, guess, create something new, try a new angle—that's what it's all about. Very few people have analyzed a market, discovered a potential product or service that may have some market pull in said market, designed an amazing business plan along with a launch strategy, scheduled the entire upcoming year or two out, launched the product, and had everything go exactly as planned. It just doesn't happen, especially for new entrepreneurs. Only after decades of experience and amazing foresight can someone launch a company with this much insight and accuracy. The world is too in flux, the markets throw too many curveballs, and there are too many variables to account for everything. That is why you must just accept the fact that along your journey you're going to fail and fail hard. And this doesn't mean only in the big picture. Like, the entire endeavor will fail, but also the small ones. In fact, especially the small ones. And by "small ones," I mean the everyday tasks that pile up over the years—the "How do I use this SEO tool?" failures; the "Is this the best type of marketing team I should hire?" failures; and the "I feel like this is a good hire for my company" failures. Constantly, consistently, you will fail. You cannot protect yourself from it. It doesn't matter how much money you have to throw at an issue, some will still surely fail. It doesn't matter how much of an education you have; there will always be something that you don't know or see that will surprise you. It doesn't matter how much experience you have building businesses;

something new and unique will always pop up. Again, it's inescapable, and you must learn to pull as much value from each failure as possible. I didn't say "learn to love failure" because I think that's stupid. You should never enjoy failing; it's a sign of incompetence or ignorance, it's a sign you did something wrong. But it's also inevitable, so take a bad thing and make it good. When life gives you failures, make failure-aid.

Every failure will give you insight. Every failure will teach you a lesson. It will teach you about your judgment, your intuition, your desires, your fears...a whole lot. It will help you uncover and discover yourself, *if* you have an open mind. Some people see failure as a bad thing and want to shelter themselves from it as much as possible. Then, when they do fail, they blame some external factor: "If it wasn't for _________, I would be doing great." Yeah, those people don't usually make it too far. You must own your failures; you must take full responsibility and accountability for your failures. As bitter as it may seem, as much as it may burn, they're yours, you own them. Now suck it up and embrace and learn from them. If you constantly blame your failures on other factors outside of your control, you will never learn from any of them. You will be living in a very closed-off world where you, in your head, know exactly what to do and exactly what's going to happen, and if it wasn't for ________ messing up your vision you would have succeeded. That's a garbage mindset, and it will get you nowhere. Accepting your failures, completely, is something you must learn to do to be a successful entrepreneur. Until you do so you'll be immobilized by your hubris and lack of humility. Thomas Edison didn't fail to create the light bulb ten thousand times. He simply learned ten thousand ways not to create a light bulb. You didn't fail to create a successful startup; you just learned one way not to go about doing it. It doesn't mean you can't try again. In fact, you must.

Okay, so how do you make the most out of failure? First, you must identify your failures. You must objectively analyze your past decisions and have an open mind and be able to identify where you screwed up. This isn't the easiest thing to do, by the way, for most people, but for you it's a piece of cake because you have a growth mindset. Many people can't accept their failures, but to learn from them, they must be discovered and critiqued. It can help tremendously if you have other people help you understand and diagnose your failures. Maybe a business partner, a spouse, a friend, anyone that has some level of knowledge about what you're up to. Anyone that can legitimately and objectively understand what you are trying to accomplish and where you failed. That can even be you. You must be critical of yourself, without getting down on yourself. It's not an easy thing to do, until you practice it enough. Once you accept that what you are doing is inherently challenging, and anybody who tried it would have a tough time, you stop being hard on yourself. What was once a feeling of failure and pessimism becomes a feeling of empowerment and trust. It might seem counterintuitive, but once you get there, you'll understand. Failure is a good thing. It's going to lift you up, if you let it.

For example, when I was working on becoming a sponsored snowboarder (something I had no business doing, as I didn't even begin snowboarding until age seventeen), I used to fall.

A lot. And I mean fall hard. Have you ever overshot a sixty-foot jump, trying to spin a 540, and landed twenty feet past the bottom of the landing? I have. Have you ever tried to do a rodeo flip and gotten stuck midair and fallen straight down on your head from twenty feet? I have. Have you ever attempted a thirty-foot cliff drop only to land and then nose-dive and rag-doll for fifty feet, with beanie and goggles strewn about the snow? I have. It sucked. I wanted to "stomp" those tricks, but they were tough, very tough. In fact, 99 percent of snowboarders weren't trying these tricks, as they were too challenging and dangerous. But you know what? I was. Because I feverishly wanted to learn how to do them. It was the coolest thing on the planet to me. I used to watch people in snowboard videos in high school do these tricks and think, "Man, that must feel so amazing," and now here I am, seven years later, trying, and sometimes landing, these exact same tricks! But it didn't come easy. There were a lot of failures, a lot of bruises, a lot of injuries, and too many concussions. But that's what it took; it was my destiny. I would take the wrath and get as good as I could. And you know what? I got pretty damn good at snowboarding. I didn't get sponsored, I never got paid to do it, but I had the time of my life and learned so much about myself I'd never change it for anything.

Yes, I lucked out. I could have been critically injured, many were, but I was strategic in my attempts and worked my way up slowly and aggressively. It's the same approach you must take as an entrepreneur. You're going to get banged up, you're going to get smashed around here and there. But ultimately, if your desire to win is greater than your fear of failure, chances are you'll succeed. It might not happen. It might not be in your cards to run a successful startup. But even if you fail, you can look around at everyone and everything and be happy and confident knowing that you busted your ass and tried to make it happen. Maybe you had a great product in a poor market. Or maybe you had the right idea five years too early. But you tried. And you didn't blame the market for it. You took full responsibility and moved on. Because you know that one day, not long from now, with the right amount of wisdom and the right amount of grinding, one of these times you're going to stomp that startup. You just have to stay optimistic, be critical of yourself in a positive and uplifting manner, and let nothing get in between you and your dreams. Nothing. Not even you.

HOW TO OVERCOME YOUR FEAR OF FAILURE:

- Write a list of your fears. What is the worst thing that can happen if your fears come true? Is it really that bad?

- Look at your project from a different angle. Set milestones for your goals. As you reach each milestone, that is a small success. If you struggle to reach a milestone, change your approach or change the milestone if it proves to be unreachable.

- Always focus on learning. If you do not meet your target, what did you learn from the process that you will do or avoid next time?

Questions for Consideration:

Do you feel you have a fear of failure? In what ways does it manifest?

What are some ways you can eliminate the fear of failure?

By when will you have this implemented?

THE VALUE OF BEING WRONG

It goes without saying, if you're going to allow yourself to fail, then you'll eventually have to admit that you were wrong about something. There's no way around it. Failure is directly correlated to being wrong about something. Whether it was a marketing campaign that cost a lot of money that brought in no revenue, or a product idea that went to market that no one wanted, or even something like expressing what you believe is a statement of fact on social media and having someone prove you wrong, you're going to be wrong. This is along the same lines as embracing your failures; you must embrace being wrong as well. It doesn't mean that you are stupid, or that you are a fool, or ignorant. It means you made a choice or drew a conclusion about something and it wasn't a good outlook. But just like with failure, as long as you admit that you are wrong and choose to move forward with the desire to better yourself from this self-admission, you will become a better, more mature person.

I'll pick an example from my own personal life. I tend to express myself a little bit too much at times. I have opinions and beliefs, and I like many of them. Also, I've been correct about many things in my life, so much so as to earn the nickname NostraDages, due to my ability to predict events with great certainty. Of course, this can lead to an elevated ego at times, and eventually I'll challenge someone on social media about something. It could be anything—market conditions, economic outlook, the price movement of an asset in the near future, a business tactic, whatever—and often I'm correct. But, of course, I'm wrong plenty of times as well. And it does hurt being wrong on a social forum, especially when the debate gets heated, as some of mine have been. I'll try to throw all the evidence I can into the conversation; I'll use ancillary information and add verifiable sources to support my position as much I can. Even then, I'm still wrong sometimes. And I'll admit it. And it sucks. But I do it to grow. Not because I enjoy it. But because I know that by admitting to my fellow debater and the world at large that I can accept being wrong, I'm able to grow from it. It's a very humbling thing to do, and though I don't like it, it has helped me a lot.

Now, I tend to be more reserved in my conversations until I know that I'm almost certainly correct. I don't get as emotional as I used to, if at all, knowing that it has led me to say stupid things that I later regretted. It still might happen, but not nearly as frequently. It also shows respect, and commands it as well. When you admit that you were wrong, most people will see that as a characteristic of strength, not weakness, and you will garner their respect in the future. If you choose to make a name for yourself and connect with people in a professional manner around the world on social media, you're going to find yourself standing up for your beliefs or opinions at some point. At least, I hope you do. We don't want a bunch of voiceless, cowardly people in our society. We need strong people who can have confidence in their knowledge and beliefs who are willing to support them on a public forum. This way we have healthy and diverse conversations amongst us all. We also need people with enough humility and desire to grow to the point that they can respect and appreciate that no one person knows everything. Being wrong is a part of the game.

Now, apply this concept to your startup. As the founder, you have some big choices to make. You often won't know if you were right or wrong in your decisions for some time. You may not pick a "failure" so to speak, but you may pick something not optimal. Surely you can think of an instance where you were speaking with a coworker or employee about a decision that had to be made. You were contemplating a few separate choices, and you went against the crowd and chose one that you thought was best, and then it turned out that it wasn't. It wasn't a flop, but say you missed out on a key opportunity, or you could have captured more profit if you would have listened to someone else and chosen a different option. Many times, when this happens, people will pretend that maybe it didn't happen, or they "weren't wrong," it's just seen differently now, or whatever lame way they try to deflect and ignore it. Doing this instead of admitting you were wrong builds bad character, if you ask me. It doesn't let people be humble. It's a way for people to try to protect themselves from the feeling of "looking stupid." They feel they need to make sure people know it wasn't them that was wrong; it was something else. Acting in this way doesn't lead to a more open office environment; it usually does the opposite. And it can easily create friction within. It's imperative that people learn how to admit they were wrong about something. It's the only way to build true respect and a cohesive team where every person's strength and weakness are discovered. It's throwing away your shield and accepting an olive branch. Some of the best leaders you'll meet will be able to do this. Of course, it will be seldom you shall see it, for they have learned from their mistakes.

Without a doubt, there is a line to be drawn here. If you're always wrong about topics, maybe you should be more reserved. If you find yourself too off-putting, maybe you should practice being more personal. If you find yourself getting emotional quickly or you make others emotional quickly, maybe you're too inflammatory and belligerent. It happens. We're humans, and it's inevitable for most of us. But you have to be willing to learn somewhere, and this may be where you start. Just be careful and realize that you must choose your battles wisely. Asserting yourself in a team environment can feel quite exposing, and you don't want to turn anyone against you. But this is your company (or these are your friends), and you're a senior member, so it's only a matter of time before someone challenges you or you find yourself in a realm of indecisiveness. You're going to have to trust yourself, ultimately, and lend your ear to others to ensure you are getting as much input about the situation as possible. Yet, eventually you'll have some tough calls to make, and eventually you'll be wrong. But if you take the initiative and admit being wrong, and have a discussion with your team about it, you'll build a better team environment, gain a lot of trust (as long as you're not wrong too often), and most importantly, learn from your mistakes and become a better entrepreneur. After all, you don't want to be one of those startup founders that is wrong a lot but never tries to accept or notice it, keeps making similar mistakes, and in the process loses the trust of the team. That's nasty. I've witnessed it firsthand. I've watched founders habitually make decisions on their own with little regard for the opinions of others, and watch those decisions fail massively.

In one such instance, a company I was working with was building up its initial inventory of durable hard goods. The choice was simple: stock up on black-colored items (the industry standard), or attempt to guess the demands of the market (with little to no real research) and make stock in multiple colors. I (and others) thought that we should go with black, because it was a safe bet and clearly the dominant color in the industry. The founder thought that they knew what people wanted and decided to stock up in three different colors. Well, those colors did not sell well and we sat on that inventory for years. To make matters worse, we had tied up a significant portion of our seed money in that inventory and couldn't sell most of it. I had to invest money to save the company and keep us moving forward. It created a negative team environment from the get-go, and we started losing employees shortly after.

HOW TO OWN YOUR MISTAKES:

- When it is brought to your attention that you have made a mistake, your first reaction, because you are human, is to cover it up. However, you need to take full responsibility for it.

- The best way to do this is in person, to the people or person you wronged or the people who were affected by your mistake.

- If you can't do it in person, a phone call is acceptable. Doing this by email will make you look like a coward, just as bad as not admitting the mistake.

- Give a sincere apology, give your reasoning for making the mistake, and ask for forgiveness.

- Moving forward, be careful not to make the same mistake again.

Questions for Consideration:

Currently, how willing do you feel you are to accept that you were wrong?

What will you gain when you accept being wrong more often, and how will you start to do so?

By when will you have this implemented?

NEUROPLASTICITY AND BEING POSITIVE

IN MY OPINION, ONE OF THE MOST FASCINATING TOPICS covered in this book is right here. How we talk to ourselves, the way we view ourselves, and our thoughts toward ourselves are everything. These things make up our reality, our worldview. Our subconscious thoughts and behaviors manifest themselves in our daily routine. They are the divining rod for our destiny. They are all we are—our thoughts, and then our subsequent actions. If we think poorly, we will act poorly. If we look at ourselves as poor, we will find poverty. It really can be that simple.

Of course, people will immediately refute this concept with the "limitations" argument. They will say that some people are born into wealthier families, others are inherently smarter, and some are just blessed with good timing.

While there may be certain instances where this is undoubtedly true, the evidence is overwhelming: how you think and speak to yourself is the biggest determinant of your life.[4] You create your reality—bottom line. Our thoughts and self-talk reshape our brains, physically. They alter our life, who we are, and how we view ourselves. You must paint a good picture of yourself, for yourself, in order for others to see you that way. Otherwise, you may show up as someone else and influence others around you to see you a certain way—not necessarily a good way.

This may sound like some over-inflated feel-good do-good false promise, whereby simply telling ourselves that we're great is some magic method that is going to make us great. Of course, it's not that easy. In fact, it is challenging. But the concept behind it all is very straightforward. Your thoughts are your reality. Think good things about yourself, consistently and honestly, and they will eventually come through. Surely, you've experienced it, in some way, shape, or form. Think back in your life to a time where you had to do something challenging or achieve some big goal. Did you do it by telling yourself that you couldn't do it? Of course not. You don't achieve things by telling yourself that you can't do them. It's possible, but rare. You achieve things by giving yourself the benefit of the doubt and trying, knowing that you may fail, and still trying your butt off because you want to do it and you know that eventually you can. And if you're going to be an entrepreneur you have to constantly believe in yourself and tell yourself that you'll figure it out. You are smart enough to make it happen. If you are not smart enough, you'll find someone who is and make it happen anyway. You deserve to be successful. You are a good person who is as capable as anybody else on Earth. Right? Yes. You must reinforce your mind with positive vibes.

After all, if you can't believe in yourself, why should anyone else? We've seen it many times, where someone is wallowing in self-doubt and misery, and someone says to them, "Hey, snap out of it. You're awesome. I've known you for years, and you can do this easily," and suddenly that strength and belief turn into an attempt and success. The only thing is that we don't always have someone there building us up. In fact, as entrepreneurs, we're alone a lot of the time, so it's critical that we learn how to build ourselves up and that we do it daily.

So how exactly does our brain retrain itself? It is said that it can take as little as three weeks (or up to eight months) to retrain our brain to form new habits.[5] Does that hold true for our thoughts? It can, if you're diligent and you back it up with proper actions. The longer you do something the deeper the channel in your brain becomes. The saying, "You can't teach an old dog new tricks," is not true at all. The issue arises because the "old dog" has its channels so deeply engrained in its brain that it seems nearly impossible to alter the neuro-pathways. But it is possible, and it happens quite often. The same goes for humans. We don't get to a point where we "can't learn new tricks"; we simply get to a point where the channels are so deep it takes a lot of time and energy to develop a new neural pathway.[6] It just takes more work to make it happen, but it can surely happen. Say you've smoked cigarettes for twenty years, and you want to quit. First off, if you say, "I'm never going to be able to quit smoking cigarettes," surely you will prove yourself right. But if you say, "I'm going to quit smoking cigarettes," and you start cutting back, you're already giving yourself a fighting chance, because you're admitting to yourself that you are capable and have the strength to quit. Now, the twenty years of formed patterns and habits will make it very tough. But over time, you'll be able to reduce consumption and ultimately quit. But without telling yourself you can, it's probably not possible. So having the conversations with yourself that reinforce your desired actions is critical.

As an entrepreneur, you'll constantly have to tell yourself how capable you are, how good you are, and how you'll figure out how to overcome the obstacle in your way, keeping you from your desired successes. After all, if you can't even tell yourself that you can do something, you're rarely going to be able to do it in practice. And for entrepreneurs, it's all practice. You can have all the knowledge in the world, but until you put it into practice, it's all conceptual. While you fail, because everyone does, you must consistently remind yourself that you will soon succeed. For that is the true secret to success in entrepreneurship, an insatiable drive to succeed and a steadfast belief in your abilities to make it work. This approach will alter and rewire your brain for success, and it is critical for your growth and progress.

WAYS TO BE MORE POSITIVE:

- Be honest with yourself when setting goals, and don't overestimate what you can do. Don't be too hard on yourself when you don't reach your targets. Tell yourself you will regroup and try again.

- Surround yourself with positive people who support you. Support them in return.

- Be thankful for the opportunity to do what you love each day. This enthusiasm will propel you forward even when things get rough.

- Acknowledge your achievements and those of your team. This will keep your morale and that of your team high and people working productively.

- Keep setting big goals for yourself and your team. Don't back down because of one failure.

- Take care of yourself mentally, physically, and emotionally. Eat right, take time off to do things you love, and exercise regularly. All of these things are simple ways to improve your outlook.

Questions for Consideration:

How do you most commonly talk to yourself now, positively or negatively?

What benefits will you gain when you start positively reinforcing yourself?

How will you start to talk to yourself more positively, and by when will you have this implemented?

ABUNDANCE MINDSET

"It's all in your head." It seems so cliché, so simple, so ridiculously basic that it can't be true. Of course, there are countless variables that dictate the success of a startup—too many to list. There are so many moving parts and interwoven elements that it's almost impossible to predict or control. There's no getting around that. But if you constantly tell yourself, "I don't have enough..." you'll surely not have enough.

This goes along with your self-talk and how you view yourself and your environment. Do you think you will succeed? Do you feel capable of succeeding? Do you have enough whatever to make it happen? Many people would quickly say "no" and then rattle off a list of many reasons why they won't succeed. And you know what? There's a lot of truth in that list. But if every entrepreneur that ever lived, from Nikola Tesla to Elon

Musk, sat there and thought about how limited they were, they probably would not have even tried. Why should they have? The odds are stacked against them, infinitely. They might as well have just gotten a job with someone else and been a general laborer working for a rich person that grew up with all the money in the world. But they didn't. They invented, they created, they solved problems, and they created a new status quo. Why? Because they grew up rich and had everything they could ever ask for? No, of course not. Because they saw unlimited potential and realized that if they could just advance their vision and project their creativity into the world, the world would provide for them. Did they always have enough money to do what they wanted? Of course not. Did they always have it all figured out? No way. Did they sit there and ruminate on what they lacked to achieve their desired outcome? Maybe. But did it stop them? Not a chance. Why? Because they knew that somewhere out there was unlimited potential: an unlimited amount of money, market demand, and resources. If only they believed in it, they would ultimately tap into it. And, surely, they did.

How much wealth is there in the world? The short answer, so much. More than you could ever fathom. Even hard cash is in the trillions. Add real estate, stocks, bonds, precious metals like gold and silver, commodities like grain and oil, cryptocurrency like Bitcoin, intellectual property rights, and so on. It's essentially infinite. Yet, you open your wallet up or check your bank account and it's not too far from a big fat goose egg, next to nothing. What gives? If there's so much money in the world, why don't you have a ton of it? Well, maybe you do, and kudos to you if that's the case, but many don't. And that's all it is. That's just the way it is right now. It's a cold, hard fact. You don't have a nice healthy piece of that money pie. But you can. You can create a revenue stream that funnels some of that cash to you. Sure, it won't be trillions, and probably not billions, maybe not even seven figures. Okay, seven figures, you're worth that easily, no sweat. But how, then—after realizing you're on the sidelines watching the money game and asking yourself, "How can I get my piece?"—do you get your piece? Well, first you must believe that you deserve a piece. Of course you deserve a piece. You're a smart, talented, dedicated person. Why shouldn't you get a piece of the pie? Well, oddly enough, many people feel they don't deserve a piece. Or can't, for whatever reason, ever get a piece. And it's true. I'll give an example.

A friend of mine, we'll call him Mike, believes that only "evil" or "bad" people get wealthy (unless they're born into wealth). That you have to "step on people's heads" to become a rich individual. Subsequently, my friend Mike is a nice guy and wouldn't ever do anything mean or evil to someone else to get ahead financially, and since that's what he believes it takes to "make it" he'll obviously never become "wealthy." In his eyes, should he ever get wealthy, it's because he used or manipulated people or somehow defied his morals to get there. It's a self-defeating approach. Clearly, Mike will never be wealthy because he's a nice guy, and nice guys don't do bad things to get rich. I don't think it takes too much thought energy to realize how false and limiting this approach is. Chances are we can all think of wealthy people who are stand-up human beings.

If you believe that you'll never have money, I'll bet you right now that you won't, aside from the incredibly rare odds that you win the lottery or inherit a fortune. Even then, you'll likely keep the same mindset and squander it all away in a few years. Why? Because that's your belief. You believe that because you live in a world of scarcity, where there "isn't enough" to go around, or you "don't deserve it" or "only evil people are rich" or whatever garbage reason you give yourself, it will never be in your cards. Well, news flash, you are just as worthy and capable as the next person, if not more so. Why? Because you are reading this and you have the desire to better yourself. That's a bigger step than most people take. Also, you're starting to realize that your scarcity mindset has taught you to see limitations everywhere. Everywhere around you are dollar signs that you can't afford. And your average job that barely pays your rent is where you max out. Unfortunately, if you believe this, you're screwed.

So, *now what*? Again, is this some "if I believe it, it will come true tomorrow" fantasy? Nope. Nothing works like that. It's a mindset shift that will take months, if not years, to come to fruition. But the first and, by far, most important step is looking at the world like, "I can add value, I am smart and capable, and there are opportunities everywhere around me where I can service the market and live very well." You must believe that. As much as you believe that you need oxygen to survive, you have to believe this. It will change the fundamental way your brain works and how you view the world. Instead of seeing limitation after limitation you'll see opportunity after opportunity. Instead of constantly seeing scarcity, you will see abundance. Will it jump out at you, simply to fall on your lap and bless you with infinite wealth? Come on now, you know better. It will take work.

You must work on first seeing the possibilities. Then you must work on understanding what skills, talents, and drive you have and start understanding what you can do, that you enjoy, to start finding a niche of some sort. It might take some soul searching and a lot of belief in yourself, which, by the way, might be the hardest part. Because up to this point you may not have believed in yourself too much. You possibly saw limitations and scarcity galore. Maybe you didn't grow up rich. Maybe you didn't go to a prestigious university. Maybe you didn't luck out and fall into a booming industry in your early twenties or so. Maybe you're just you. And paying your cell phone bill, car insurance, rent, and everything else you need to survive is already a pain in the butt, and you can't see a way out of it. But you're an entrepreneur. You have drive. You want more.

So, how do you go about getting more? Well, the first step is to look at the world like an oyster opening up and showing off a beautiful pearl, just for you. This is opposed to seeing the world as a Venus flytrap where you're the fly and the trap is society. You must reverse that. Instantly. And if you don't, then you are cementing your future in a scarcity mindset. Do you know how many people there are who may be less intelligent than you, less charismatic than you, and less driven than you who have gone on to start and build highly successful businesses? The short answer: a ton, more than worth trying to comprehend. You want to know how they did it? It's simple: they found a niche, something they enjoyed, created a good or service to support it, believed in themselves, and worked their butts off. Did everyone succeed? No way, not a chance. Many failed. Many died poor and struggling, like most of the nine-to-five office grinders who never even gave it a shot. They may not have gotten the results they were looking for, but you know what? At least some gave it a shot. And the ones that did had at least some level of self-belief and courage to try. Thankfully, many were successful. Many went on to become very wealthy and very happy. Yeah, sure, it was a numbers game. Some were bound to succeed and others bound to fail. For the sake of simple math, let's just use the Pareto principle, the 80/20 rule, and say that for every one hundred people that tried to become successful entrepreneurs, eighty failed and went right back to their previous type of employment at wherever. And twenty of those one hundred people built successful startups, of many different types. Were some super smart? Of course. Were some not so intelligent? Yep. But they all believed that there was a bigger piece of the pie out there for them that they could go get. Some got it, and some did not. Well, you're no different. Ultimately, we're all a statistic of some sort—a number, a data trail that leaves notes everywhere we go. But you are also you. And you are also driven. And you want that "dash" in between your birthdate and your death date to represent more than just the usual life—the standard and predictable trail of data points. If anything, you'll at least give it a shot, a shot to mix it up and live better. And it's in this shot that you must see infinite abundance. It's the abundance attitude that will help you move forward. It's the abundance attitude that will let you see the opportunities you did not see before.

This will apply everywhere you take it. Seeing abundance is a daily exercise. It's not just in a few random moments. In a way, it's the "Is the glass half full or half empty?" approach. When you go to the bank to withdraw money, do you think to yourself, "Oh man, am I just always going to be spending money?" or do you think, "Cool I have this much money to do X with and the rest to make more things happen"? It could be $200, or it could be $20,000, but the approach is the same. For when you see things as "half full," you see that it is an additive process. It is "full" or "filling up," which means that things are being added to it. Yeah, sure, you took $500 out of $20,000 total, but that $20,000 is growing. You're making it. And it's not a negative thing; it's just a small financial subtraction from an ever-growing pie. But if you're the "glass half empty" type, then you're taking a subtractive approach, one where you have dwindling amounts and you are just constantly watching your reserves get lower. Sometimes you do this to the point where you fixate on it yet can't seem to alter the direction of the movement. Why is that? Why do we do that sometimes? For some of us, it's in our programming. We focus on what we're losing instead of what we're gaining. But you can change that. You can choose to look for, and believe in, abundance. Abundance in your sales of your good or service. Abundance in your financial well-being and startup capital. Abundance in the help and assistance you get from other people. Abundance in your ability to learn whatever skills you may need along the way to grow the business. Abundance in the network of the industry to grow and make great connections. You have to see everything as abundance and possibility. Only then will doors open for you. The bottom line is you find what you look for, and when you look for scarcity, you find it. When you look for abundance, you find it. You must get out of your own way if you want to succeed. Because, after all, the only person stopping you from succeeding is you. You may not believe it. It may take way longer than you want it to. But believing that there is abundance out there for you is a critical step to take in finding it and making it yours.

HOW TO CREATE AN ABUNDANCE MINDSET:

- Practice gratitude. When you start to see all the good around you and are thankful for what is already in your life, it is easy to see that there is more than enough, and it is right at your fingertips.

- Believe that you can do anything you set your mind to. Your mindset is a big part of your success. You can only do it if you believe you can.

- Choose your thoughts and words carefully. What you say and what you think are very powerful influences in the world. By filtering out the negative and only thinking the positive, you will experience a lot more good in your life.

- Your positivity will rub off on those around you—so will your negativity, so choose wisely.

Questions for Consideration:

Do you currently see the glass as half full or half empty?

How would your life change if you started to see things more positively?

How will you do this, and by when will you have this implemented?

LIFE IS ABOUT HUMAN CONNECTION

OF COURSE, IT'S NOT POSSIBLE TO BUILD A THRIVING STARTUP or business without other people being there with you. There's no way around it. You only exist in other human beings. You're not going to sell your widget to a bird, or a dog. You're going to sell it to other humans. You're going to source your supplies from people. Rely on other people to help share and build your vision. Hang out with and learn about other people in your industry. You're going to be surrounded by people, so you should learn to appreciate that fact. You don't necessarily have to enjoy it all the time. You're not forced to put on a fake smile just because you're with someone, though you must, at the least, appreciate the fact that you only exist in other human beings. You really can't go that far without other people.

Your name only exists in other people. Your dog doesn't know your first and last name, what you do for work, and what your business is all about. All your dog knows is that you're the pack leader, you bring it food and water, you call the shots, and your dog helps keep you happy. It doesn't identify you as a "human," nor does it understand what's going on. It can never pay you monetarily for services or help you move forward in the marketplace. Only humans can. Only humans can help you advance in the world of humans. Everything you do in your business is with humans. It's for a human, by a human, and surely, financed by a human. Think about everything you do in your average week. From the minute you wake up to the minute you go to bed. I'm willing to bet that every single task you do involves a human. You wake up in a house built by humans. You eat breakfast produced by humans. You drive to work in a car produced by humans. You work and get paid by humans. And so on and so forth. Taking it one step further, beyond mere consumerism, you're an entrepreneur, you're offering up a solution or advancement in some area. You must work with and talk to other people to build that up. There's no way around it. People are your lifeblood. We are all connected. We all need each other.

This a great thing, actually, as one of the leading causes of depression is loneliness. Being isolated from others is a contributing cause of depression and other mental ailments.[7] It really is important for your mental health to allow yourself to be engaged with others. Opening oneself up to the world and people is an enlightening event. Although you may not necessarily be the type, it's definitely worth the effort. It's good for all of us too. Society can be so closed off, so at odds especially in times like now, where there is great uncertainty and cultural confusion.

The best way to reverse this is by accepting and appreciating the fact that we truly only exist in other human beings. It's a brave and rewarding concept, although it can be a bit scary, especially for introverts like me. I love my alone time. I spend most of my time alone, in fact. I enjoy going out, but I don't really enjoy random conversations with strangers. I'd rather stick to myself and save the awkward small talk for never. Don't bother me, and I won't bother you. But it's a limiting approach, especially for an entrepreneur. Entrepreneurs are in constant discover-and-create mode, always looking for an opportunity or a new product or service idea. Some of us can spend weeks in our head analyzing and attempting to figure out new things or find new approaches. And it's good; we need to be able to do this to create. Nikola Tesla once said, "Be alone, that is the secret of invention; be alone, that is when ideas are born." But once the invention is created, there is a world of humans to show it off and market it to, and that's where the fun begins.

By showing humility and sympathy, smiling, and engaging in small talk with others, you create a deeper connection. People will remember you as someone genuine that stands out. You'll foster more friendships, better relationships, improved mental health, and just feel better about probably almost everything in your life (sounds dramatic, but it might just make a world of difference for you). So, make the effort and reach out to others. Enjoy our humanity and our commonalities. (Despite what the media says, we all are far more alike than we are different.) Unity is something we desperately need right now, and it will also help your organization grow stronger, faster, and better.

HOW TO CREATE MORE HUMAN CONNECTION:

- When you walk by someone in the hall, say, "Hello, how are you?"

- Give people fist-bumps or high-fives if that is your style. If it isn't, consider making it your style, or a friendly handshake or wave will do.

- Make eye contact with people and smile.

- Ask coworkers how their weekends were, how their family is doing, how their vacation was, how their favorite ball team is doing.

- Go even further and reach out to your vendors and customers and just ask them how their business is doing. Ask if they have any concerns you can help them with, what you can do to help them out, and if anything is missing from your partnership.

These seemingly small but valuable gestures can make a huge difference, in you and them.

Questions for Consideration:

What currently keeps you from connecting with others effectively?

What would be the benefits of connecting with people more?

How will you do this, and by when will you have this implemented?

STAKEHOLDERS, NOT JUST SHAREHOLDERS

ONE OF MY MOST FAVORITE ELEMENTS OF THE B CORP certification model is that they emphasize the "stakeholders not shareholders" approach to business. This differs from the traditional corporate model where "shareholder primacy is of utmost importance," which essentially is saying, "Increase the value for shareholders above everything else." This is a dangerous, myopic, and selfish approach to business, and corporations are beginning to shun it. It doesn't take much thought to realize how many people a corporation affects daily. Shouldn't we focus on more than just making money for the shareholders? Of course we should. We should be looking at not only making money for the company but also ensuring that our company is adding value to the world far beyond accumulating money. After all, an unsustainable business model is, ultimately, unsustainable. Now, more than ever, consumers are focused on their morals and values when it comes to how they spend their money. You may have a great product at a highly competitive price, but if your company is creating massive pollution, you will see environmentally conscious consumers turn their back on you and purchase a product from a more expensive yet environmentally minded company. This is a trend that is advancing at breakneck speed, so I advise that you get your firm on board.

It can be challenging to determine what your firm's impact will be on all of the stakeholders involved. After all, a stakeholder is anyone and everyone affected by your corporation. That's a lot of people. That's everyone involved in supplying your products and those sourcing them. That's all your customers, your landlord, and even the electric company you use. It's the waste management system you rely on to handle and eliminate your waste. It's everyone that is affected, in any way, shape, or form, by the existence of your company. It can be very challenging to list out who all these people are, because many of them will be outside of the scope of your realization. But when forming a business and understanding how you want your self-expression received by the world, it's a great opportunity to address these issues early on. This will serve as part of your direction and mentality as you build your business. For it is much harder to implement changes in your firm once you are established and running full-steam ahead.

You have practices and procedures already in place. You have policies and supply chains already developed. It'll be much easier for you to slightly adjust your course when you're just starting out of the gates versus when you are in a full sprint. So, let's take the time to look at and understand how you can take a stakeholder-focused view of your firm without overwhelming yourself.

Start with your core product or service. What does it do? How does the delivery of the service or the manufacturing of the product impact your stakeholders? Does it do so in a negative or positive way? Is this something that creates more pollution, waste, or toxic by-products? Do you have to import components from all over the world to make it? Is there an excessive amount of energy to get it to you? Could this be something procured domestically, with a slightly higher price but with a lower environmental footprint? These are some things to consider when understanding how your company's services affect others. Does it help or hurt your stakeholders?

For example, let's take a product that is relatively easy to make, has locally sourced raw inputs, has a low environmental footprint, is primarily used to clean oil stains off the pavement, and does so in the safest and least toxic way yet. This would be something that right out of the gate affects stakeholders positively. It does more than simply provide a revenue stream. It positively impacts many stakeholders everywhere and would be good for the environment too.

Now let's take a durable good, some type of sporting equipment or something. It's made out of PVC plastic, which is toxic, and it has components shipped from around the world that are to be aggregated at the main facility in the US and then repackaged as complete, only to be sent back out around the world. That has a much bigger environmental footprint and creates toxic by-products, and the product itself would have a negative impact on many of the stakeholders. If this is your product, maybe you want to second-guess either the industry or the product itself, or look at ways to make it better, to reduce the environmental footprint and have less toxic by-products. Because after all, not all stakeholders are people. The earth can be, and usually is, a stakeholder. So are the animals of the ocean and the air we breathe.

Stakeholder analysis takes a holistic view of what you do. It is critical when building your foundation that you spend some time really understanding what you're willing to compromise to get to your destination. Some people simply do not care about anything other than themselves and their goals and don't even spend a minute thinking about their stakeholders. Some people will quickly toss away a great potential product because it violates their personal code of ethics or their morals. Which type of person are you? Chances are you're like neither of the two types mentioned, but likely identify somewhere in between. You don't want to disregard everyone and everything else just to make some money, but you're also willing to bend some personal rules if it means you'll get to live the successful lifestyle you desire.

It is important that you analyze this, because when it's all said and done, this is your legacy.

Taking this holistic approach is becoming more and more appreciated. Of course, it is very tough. But don't let that dissuade you. I think you'll find it relaxing and empowering when you analyze the impact your company will have and make conscientious decisions to make changes for the better. It can inspire you and inspire others as well. You might even sleep better knowing that you're taking part in this game of capitalism, trying to live your best life, while also being a decent and well-intentioned person. It's not a good feeling when you have to constantly wonder if your products are killing animals in the ocean, or creating a toxic by-product that is harming other people, or even just using excessive energy and creating waste when you know they don't have to. And don't be misled; this type of approach in your business will not hinder your progress. In fact, it may propel you. As you talk with potential clients/customers, an energy of optimism and positivity will come over you. These are talking points that you will love sharing. This is good conversation and network building. The people you interact with will feel your enthusiasm, your good intent, and the fact that you are, in fact, taking the bull by the horns and shaping a future of intent and purpose. You're not just another "businessperson" doing whatever you can to make some money. You're an intentional creator, driven by your purpose and values, and you have an excellent foundation to work with and truly care about everything and everyone your company or organization affects. Which is quite admirable.

HOW TO CONSIDER STAKEHOLDERS OVER SHAREHOLDERS:

- First, find out what is most important to you, your team, and your clients. Is it the environment, fair wages for workers, a reduced carbon footprint, sustainability, or other things?

- Then, take a hard look at your vendors, your business, and your customers. Is your product or service considering the stakeholders throughout its life cycle, from the source to what happens after it is no longer useful to the end customer?

- Consider what can be done to make it so. Make sure your stakeholders know what you are doing and why.

Questions for Consideration:

Are you currently putting stakeholders or shareholders first?

What are some of the benefits of putting stakeholders first?

How will you do this in your startup, and when will you have this implemented?

EVERYONE NEEDS A PIECE

One of the hardest things for a founder to do is give up a piece of their business. It's their self-expression and a reflection of themselves. Not to mention, once you give any of it away, chances are you're not going to get it back, so you want to be sure of the people you include in the ownership. But also, you don't want to be completely alone, do you? You want a team, to have people involved in your company that are passionate and have a real reason to help you build your vision. So, while it might seem like giving away some ownership to employees is a bad idea, it's probably the best thing you can do to incentivize people to grind through it with you. After all, would you rather own 100 percent of a business that's worth nothing or 30 percent of a business that's worth millions? Seems pretty obvious to me.

One of the main aspects of the B Corp/certification model is the big emphasis on allocating a good percentage of the ownership to employees. Usually somewhere around 40 percent of the overall ownership is what they recommend. That is essentially suggesting that 40 percent of all corporate shares be allocated for employees of the company, to increase morale and create more drive for the employees. An employee who is working forty hours a week only to take home a paycheck likely won't be that driven. Especially if you are still in the early stages of your startup, money is tight, and you are unable to pay employees in a competitive manner. In fact, many startups do not offer any benefits or bonuses because the first few years are generally very tight financially. So now you have employees that aren't making that much money, not receiving any benefits, getting weak (if any) annual bonuses, have no ownership in the company, and are working at a startup that might not even make it in the long run. Meanwhile, you have the lion's share of the ownership and are probably taking the biggest paycheck in the company, because you're CEO and owner. It wouldn't be too surprising if many, if not all, of your employees are looking to move onto a bigger and better company.

People want to be a part of something big, something they can be proud of. Remember, they are working for your self-expression, creating your dream, and not getting much for it in return. That sucks. I would never want to own a company where my employees were so poorly treated and the ownership base was that lopsided (I've walked away from companies for this reason). Also, having the corporate say so intensely focused in the hands of one or only a few members creates a tunnel-vision type of approach where there is a lack of input and only a small amount of diversity in the focus of the firm. From my experience, companies owned by a small group or the founder don't do that well only because they don't have enough collaboration and insight when moving forward. I've watched potentially very good startups decay from the inside out because the ownership was hoarded by the family and the majority of the decision-making of the company was too consolidated. It destroyed morale, it created a lack of enthusiasm, and there were many mistakes and oversights because there was a massive lack of team input and collaboration. It is pretty disheartening.

Of course, you don't want to give random employees ownership either, because once it's given, it cannot be taken back. It's important to make sure that you are not giving ownership to anyone who is not fully committed to the success of the company. Make sure they are committed for the long haul. Include a vesting period so they stay at the company for a certain number of years before they receive the ownership. Then, after that, place contingencies around the sale of the ownership. Make sure they cannot sell to competitors or anyone who may be of poor character. For example, they cannot sell to people convicted of financial crimes, as one example. The good thing is that these rules are essentially all up to you, so it's your call as to what the parameters are. Just be sure to set limitations and make sure that you spend time considering this. Once you hand over ownership it's permanent, but it can also be very beneficial for the overall health of the company.

So, what's a good way to structure this? Well, of course, there are a few ways to do it, but I recommend something that has a number of shares allocated per year for a few years. For example, let's say there are one million shares issued. You sign on someone and agree that they get one thousand shares for every year they work there, for five years. They can't sell the ownership until at least one year after they receive it. So, at the end of year one of their employment, they get one thousand shares, but cannot sell them until the end of year two. They don't have to keep their job there; say they move out of state or something one and a half years in and they still have their initial one thousand shares. They get to keep the original one thousand shares but cannot gain any more, of course, and must wait until the end of year two to sell. Don't forget, this is more than likely a private company, so selling shares won't be anywhere near as easy as selling shares of a public company on the open market. But regardless, it's good to have ownership, and many companies are appreciating holding private company stock over public company stock these days for many reasons.

Again, this is just an example. Talk to a certified public accountant (CPA) or certified management accountant (CMA) about it when you structure the company to decide how many shares you want to issue and what percent you want to allocate for employees. Then, you can understand better how many chunks you want to allocate and for which types of employees, as well as how you want to release the shares. There are many ways to go about doing this, of course, so have fun with it. Create a system that is enjoyable, keeps people inspired to help you build the company, and gives them the hope that maybe one day your startup will hit it big and they'll have an amazing investment from it. It's that long-term hope that keeps people driving forward beyond their paycheck and possible lack of benefits.

HOW TO GIVE EVERYONE A PIECE OF THE COMPANY:

- Decide how you will give people a piece of the prosperity. Will you issue shares of the company, bonuses for profits, or profit sharing?

- Put it in writing, and then make sure you deliver on your promise.

- Tweak the plan as necessary to ensure that people are getting a fair share.

- Backdate the plan for older employees if you feel it is more fair to do so.

Questions for Consideration:

Major obstacles to giving every employee some equity:

How can you most easily and effectively give everyone a piece?

By when will you have this implemented?

OVER/UNDER CONFIDENCE

THIS IS ONE OF THE HARDEST THINGS TO UNDERSTAND AND control about being an entrepreneur: the balance of confidence. Of course, if you have the courage to start your own business you must have a good deal of confidence in yourself. However, too much confidence can really cause you to struggle. Inversely, too little confidence, which many people have, can also create obvious issues. Let's look into this more.

Overconfidence is when you have, well, too much confidence. Some people may call it bravado, or it could manifest itself as ego. Regardless, being too confident can be detrimental for you and your startup. Overconfident founders generally have a difficult time asking others for help. Or they tend to think their decisions are the best, disregarding others' ideas. They have a hard time taking criticism from other people, because they think they are doing everything great. It can show up in many ways and ultimately leads to a type of tunnel-vision approach where the founder is solely reliant on their decisions. This can also cause an overconfident founder to shut out their employees when it comes to decision-making, or not even listen to them at all. They may act like they are listening when in fact they are not. Or, they may listen to other people's ideas and decisions only to instantly disregard them and then later down the road, if it in fact was a good decision, make it seem like they thought of it themselves. This may or may not be deliberate, but it happens a lot. I've witnessed it firsthand many times and it drives team members absolutely crazy.

I've been a victim of this. I've made numerous recommendations over the years to business partners only to have them shot down immediately and disregarded. Then, maybe a year or two later when said person finally "got" what I was suggesting and why I was suggesting it, they seemed to come up with the same idea, but anew, and from their own mind. It drove me nuts. I've also seen it happen to numerous employees I've worked with and it has likely happened to you. It can be rough. A founder who doesn't listen to their employees can often hear the idea and subconsciously "store" it in their brain, and then when the same scenario comes up again they are like, "Hey, I have a great idea," only to regurgitate someone else's idea from months if not years ago. It creates tension within the company. It leaves employees feeling like they are not a part of the decision-making process. It may even make someone feel disrespected and like their idea was stolen. It's not a good trait to have by any means and it will whittle away your team's faith in you to be a good leader. If anything, you'll look like a know-it-all who steals other people's ideas.

My recommendation is to avoid doing this. Take the insight from Lesson 4 and listen genuinely to your employees. When they have a good idea give them credit where credit is due. Then, if that situation arises again and the said idea becomes useful, have the courage to appreciate the person for making the recommendation years ago. It'll show some respect and build some appreciation, usually on both ends.

Another pitfall from overconfidence is not recognizing you need to add skilled employees to the team to move things forward faster and better. I've seen founders who thought they could figure out whatever they needed despite having little or no college experience, little or no business-building experience, and little or no know-how in a field. The whole "create from nothing" approach can be great for some things, and is necessary for entrepreneurs, but there's a lot to be said for hiring people who already have skills and talents, knowledge, and know-how. Your company will need these people for future growth and to understand exactly what all you're involved in. When a founder doesn't want to hire someone who can help catapult the company forward with their knowledge and skills and simply thinks that "we can figure this out on our own," it can cost the company massive opportunities and delay growth for years.

It's best not to be so overconfident in your ability to figure it out as you go and hire the people you need when you need them. Your business will grow faster and you'll have an empowered team. This is preferred over the other alternative: hiring entry-level employees that you must train yourself. Oftentimes you'll be training them on things you just learned and knew nothing about months ago. Not to mention it's likely something that you just learned through a quick online search and now you think you're an "expert" and you're trying to teach it to others as well. But keep in mind, the source that you learned it from likely has years of education or experience and they know all the technical nuances that you, the founder, do not. Of course, for many things, you have to learn as you go, but if you are "learning as you go" for every single element of your startup it's going to take you much longer to get to profitability, or you might be losing employees because you're moving too slowly. Do your best and have the courage to hire someone who can help launch your company forward without burdening your finances too much. Because constantly shooting from the hip every day, every week, and every month can really drag down overall performance. It's a great way to sputter and waste time—not only yours, but your teammates' as well.

Now, for the obvious one: underconfidence. There are many clear reasons why being underconfident can cause problems in your startup. Underconfidence may lead to a lack of trust in your own judgment. Lack of confidence can lead to indecision, and have you spend too much time pondering different possibilities. Lack of confidence can manifest itself as aggression or anger because you are constantly battling with yourself and your lack of feeling sure of yourself. Other employees may see your lack of confidence and begin doubting your abilities to lead or manage, which can create division within the team. If this is the case, the first thing you must do is start building up your confidence. You already have enough faith in yourself to launch a startup, so now you just need to bump it up a little bit, and you're good to go. A great way to do this is to challenge yourself in ways that are achievable but not easy. Set goals for yourself that you immediately think you cannot do, but after a short internal deliberation, realize are definitely possible.

If public speaking is one of the places where your lack of confidence manifests itself, and it's a business priority, take the time to practice. Practice at home by yourself. Practice at your company with a handful of employees, growing more and more of an audience as you go. You could join Toastmasters or something similar where you get a lot of help and assistance from others who are out to do the same as you: develop more confidence, and become a better speaker. There are many ways to build confidence and the more you work at it the stronger it will become. It's just one of those things that some people naturally have and others don't. But if you're going to take the company to the stars, you must have a good level of confidence in yourself. If you don't have that, you must work on developing it. Just make sure you don't *overdevelop* it.

It's clear that the confidence balance is a fine line. You need to have enough confidence to make decisions that boldly attack entrepreneurship, but too much and you may come off as egotistical and myopic, trusting only your decisions and no one else's. This can leave you isolated and without sufficient external input to help you grow intelligently. Most entrepreneurs have an abundance of or too much confidence, as belief in oneself is a key ingredient to the entrepreneurial mindset. But it's not uncommon to see someone who has a great idea, someone who maybe wants to be an entrepreneur, stand paralyzed with indecisiveness and lack of confidence. This is a balance you will surely develop over time. The main thing is to be aware of it. Many entrepreneurs would not believe that too much confidence is possible. But it definitely can be, and it can surely hamper growth. Good teams have good leaders that are confident enough to take the reins but also not so overconfident that they don't know when to hand them off. It takes a team, and it's all about balance.

HOW TO GET A GOOD BALANCE OF CONFIDENCE:

- Write down your strengths and your weaknesses. What things are you good at, what things do you enjoy doing, and what things are you highly educated in?

- Find out what things your team excels at and enjoys doing.

- Are there things you are currently doing or want to do that your team would be more skilled at doing?

- Think about delegating those tasks so you can focus on what you are the best at. Spend time building up your strengths and also weaknesses that you think you can improve.

Questions for Consideration:

On a scale of one to ten, with one being the lowest, how confident do you think you currently are?

In what ways would boosting your confidence up a few points help you and your startup?

What areas can you work on to further boost your confidence, and when will you have this implemented?

THE VALUE OF COMPLETION

It's quite often that we have many different projects happening at once. At times there are so many projects that we tend to lose track of whether they are finished or what stage of the process they are in. It's not uncommon to completely lose track of the progress of projects and have them dropped altogether. This is why, as we discussed in the Lesson 3, it's critical to keep a schedule to ensure that you are filling your week with productivity and doing your best not to forget anything.

However, projects can drag on, or take days or weeks to accomplish. Sometimes you'll get halfway through something and it may take a few days or a week or so to be able to get back to it. Every incomplete project is another "thing" that you have lingering in the back of your mind. Give it a good think. How many incomplete projects do you have right now? How many incomplete conversations with other people do you have right now? There's probably a long list of incompletions that exist in your life. From hobby projects that you want to complete, to conversations with friends and coworkers that you left open-ended, to professional tasks that may be scattered all over the place, you have a brain full of incomplete tasks.

To put this in a way that may make some more sense, imagine your laptop, desktop, or smartphone, where you have a bunch of different web pages open, an app or two open, and maybe some other background tasks running as well. How well does your computer function when it's juggling a bunch of different jobs? Not that well. It gets sluggish. It can be slow. While it's trying to make one app or tool work well there are other ones that need to pull computing power, so it takes away from the primary task. When you have half a dozen or more of these running, you'll realize that your computer runs very slowly. So slow sometimes that you have to shut everything down and reboot the computer so it can clean itself out again and start fresh.

Well, your brain is the same. But immensely more complicated. It takes a massive amount of computing power from your brain for you to simply exist—to juggle all your biological functions, take in all the inputs from your environment and make sense of them, avoid danger at all costs, and finally, have consciousness and be a functioning, interactive human. But despite all that going on in the background you still find a way to complicate your brain more.

I remember a time when I was working long hours and had little time to do anything in my personal life. I would try to get all kinds of stuff done, with several projects going all at once, and I promised people things that I never made my way back around to, or just forgot about completely. I wasn't getting enough sleep, I was stressed, and everything started to suffer. I made silly mistakes, which cost me even more time, and I couldn't come up with the words for what I wanted to say when I wanted to say them, which made me a less effective leader. When I did focus on a project, I felt like I couldn't focus on it completely, so it took longer. It was just a domino effect of poor time management and I knew I couldn't go on that way. I had to stop, regroup, do one thing at a time, and then only take on what I could comfortably do at one time from then on out. And you know what? I actually got more done that way!

The first step in getting your tasks complete is to get them to a point where no more work can be done on them. It sounds simple, but it can be confusing. For me, there are two stages of completion, TSOC and PSOC. TSOC is a *temporary state of completion*, whereas PSOC is a *permanent state of completion*. TSOC is where you have gotten to a point where you can no longer do any more work, but the project isn't fully done yet. Maybe you are waiting on additional parts to arrive in a few days, or maybe you have finished your part of the project and have handed it off to another person to finalize and complete. It's in a temporary state of completion, but needs to be followed up on and eventually put in the PSOC category. Something that is PSOC, that has a permanent state of completion, is done and done. The task, or conversation, or project, is 100 percent done, and you can forever check it off your list of things to do.

Let's look at some examples.

Let's say you task an employee with a report on something in your company. It's Monday and you expect it to be handed to you by Wednesday for your review. Wednesday comes and you are given the report, and it is in a TSOC, because you have to review and make sure that it covers all the details you need. For the employee that handed you the paper it is also TSOC, as they cannot do anything more until you send it back, but it's not fully completed. Once it has been returned with your requested edits you can consider it TSOC and wait for the finalized version to be sent back to you. The employee will take your suggested edits and apply them and they can be in a PSOC, as they have revised the paper and given it back to you in a completed state. You review the paper, take what you need from it, and file it away for good. Done and done.

That was a simple and obvious TSOC/PSOC explanation. Let's make one a little more obscure. Most of us have employee issues in our company. Maybe you don't like the way a certain person talks in your company, or maybe there are double standards. One place I've seen this many times is the company break room. The company refrigerator can be a very useful yet troubling area. Some people bring food and put it in the fridge, and others may take some of it without permission, leaving people upset. Some people may complain about other people leaving their food in the fridge for too long, to the point where it goes bad, time and time again, only to not realize they do it more than anyone else. I've seen this play out, and it's quite comical.

One person constantly complains to others about old food in the fridge, but then they leave a sandwich or something in there for a month. Everyone in the company knows whose sandwich it is, because of the composition, and everyone is irked and angered that the one time they forget some food in the fridge they get reprimanded, but the person that is doing the reprimanding is the primary culprit. The person that got reprimanded is "incomplete" about this entire scenario because he sees hypocrisy and double standards. But instead of respectfully confronting the other person about it, he just tries to forget about it. He puts it in the TSOC category and attempts to move on and force it into the PSOC category. But he can't. It's in the back of his head, and every time he sees something in the fridge that's been left for too long, or that same person lectures someone else about leaving food in the fridge, he is reminded of the hypocrisy.

This matter can eat away at most people, cause them to harbor resentment, and create a feeling of distrust. It can be a very negative energy for the company, and it will compound if not resolved. So, you must resolve it. You must create a state of completion with this, and you do that by telling the person that you do not appreciate their lack of integrity and hypocrisy. You must get it off your chest because it will take over space in your mind and keep you from focusing on other important things. So, have the chat. Or have multiple team members have the chat. I would be willing to bet that this person is ignorant most of the time they do it and will try to correct this bad habit. Hopefully they do, and that's the end of it. The gripe will be completed, and it will no longer exist. This is much better than letting it linger within the team, compounding with negative energy. If the person fails to correct their bad habit of leaving their food in the fridge for too long and still lectures others when they do it, you may just have to accept that they are a hypocrite and try to avoid them. These types of people can be toxic, and it may be best to find a work-around so you don't have to be in constant conflict with them, as chances are they take this behavior everywhere they go.

Resolving issues like this and creating completion can be tough. Incompletions can reach back years if not decades and be in many places you may not expect. They can manifest in the form of a conversation that is not finished, or a task that is still lingering, or a goal you never accomplished, and it is best to take a survey of your life and list out as many of your incompletions as possible and start checking them off. Once this is done, your brain will be freed up, and you will be able to focus and function much more efficiently.

HOW TO COMPLETE TASKS:

- Make a list of all the things you have to do. Include everything, down to unanswered emails and very small tasks.

- Do not make plans for any new tasks until you get these current tasks done.

- Start with the smallest tasks, those that will only take a minute or two, and get them done first. When you get all of these small tasks marked off your list, your load will feel a lot lighter, and you will have some good momentum.

- At this point, you can start answering emails again, but do not leave any unanswered. Stay on top of them as you finish your larger tasks.

- Now, tackle the large tasks one at a time until you are done with them all.

- Once everything is completed, you can start to add new projects to your plate, but be sure to answer all your emails, return messages, and complete projects one at a time from here on out. Delegate any other projects as needed. Saying no is your friend, and you will be a lot more effective if you work this way.

Questions for Consideration:

Do you currently have mounds of uncompleted tasks you need to complete? How does that affect your productivity and mindset?

How would getting a clean slate with your tasks and then taking on one task at a time until completion, either permanent or temporary, feel and benefit you?

How will you start to implement this, and by when will you have this implemented?

THE NEGATIVE IMPACT OF GOSSIP

IN STARTUPS YOUR TEAM IS USUALLY VERY SMALL AND TIGHT-knit. If you're in a larger organization, chances are that you still work in somewhat siloed smaller groups. Each relationship becomes quite personal quite quickly as you work with each other building your company. Therefore, it's incredibly important that you maintain a strong sense of team and stay positive. But ultimately conflict will arise. People will get angry at others for certain things, and eventually, people will probably start talking smack and gossiping about each other. This can be devastating for your startup.

To be clear, let's look at exactly what gossip is and is not. According to the Merriam-Webster definition, gossip is when "a person habitually reveals personal or sensational facts about others." Gossip is, very plainly, talking bad about someone behind their back and disclosing personal facts about them in a derogatory way. And it does nothing good for the team. And to be frank, we've probably all done it before. I know I have, even knowing how much it can harm a team. But it only breeds negativity. It's not good by any means. Gossip is not constructive criticism. It is not respectfully confronting others and telling them your concerns or attempting to solve a problem.

Gossip is something that you must not allow to live in your company. You need a team of people where mutual respect is abundant and positivity oozes throughout. A team where, when people have problems with others, you bring it to light and make sure that it is discussed and completed once and for all. You can't afford to have people being negative to others and creating decay in your company. Because that's what gossip is, it's a form of decay. It will create an environment of distrust and disrespect, so find a way to prevent it, and if it does occur, get rid of it quickly. It's fairly simple to accomplish this.

HOW TO END GOSSIP IN YOUR BUSINESS:

- Make a company policy on gossip and decide on how repeat offenders will be handled. An example would be, the first and every offense, the gossiper and person they gossiped about will be brought together to hash out the issue. The second offense, the gossiper will be sent home without pay, and the third offense, the gossiper will be fired, or as you see fit.

- When starting your company, or hiring new people, make it very clear that gossip will not be tolerated and that if someone gossips, they will be disciplined according to the policy. Tell them there is no room in your company for gossip. You're here to build a strong team full of good values and mutual respect.

- Make sure to follow through each and every time. By doing so, you will create a stronger workplace where your employees get along better and are more productive, and you will very effectively curb any type of gossiping.

Questions for Consideration:

In what ways is your company currently suffering due to the gossip and strained relationships of people?

How can you most easily and valuably eliminate gossip?

By when will you have this implemented?

AVOID DOUBLE STANDARDS AT ALL COSTS

DOUBLE STANDARDS CAN HAVE SUCH A NEGATIVE IMPACT on an organization. They can be just as destructive as gossip. They can whittle away a team's trust in each other and create continual cycles of tension and animosity. To be clear, a double standard is basically when a person expects certain behaviors of others while excusing themselves from the requirement, either consciously or unconsciously. An example of a double standard could be a boss telling their employees that they all must arrive at 8:00 a.m. sharp for work every day, and then the same boss strolling in whenever he chooses. Or a boss constantly telling their employees to keep their work-time conversations focused on work throughout the day, but yet they talk about something not work-related for half of the day. This is akin to not keeping one's word. It's not exactly saying one thing and doing another, but more so instructing others to follow one rule and then not following it yourself.

This may affect the team by making your employees feel like they are your subjects, like there are two sets of rules for people to follow. One set is for one group of people, the subjects, and one is for another set of people, the ruler and his or her favorites. It can be seen or construed as "bourgeoisie versus proletariat," where there is "management" and then there are "the laborers." Usually the laborers far outnumber management, and usually this leads to more people being upset than content.

People can frequently lash out in rebellion or begin to purposely disobey orders because they feel as if the owner/manager thinks they are "below" him or her, or that they are subjugated to certain rules not meant for everyone. This can lead people to feel like they are simply "the worker" while the boss gets all the benefits of the company. When you think about this, it makes sense. The manager/boss usually always makes more money than the laborers, usually has a more comfortable office area and workspace, usually has more flexibility in their day and schedule, and usually gets more benefits from the company at large. So, it makes it even that much more of a rub in the face when the manager tells people that the team has to stick to a certain set of rules or guidelines but then goes out and, like a hypocrite, does the opposite. Employees don't like that. It makes them feel taken advantage of and sometimes "like a slave." It's one of those things that must be avoided at all costs, just like gossip.

Let's look at how to structure your guidelines and such to limit animosity on your team.

A great way to build an organization that is clear of double standards is to start easy. Don't put too many restrictions or rules into place that you immediately know you won't follow. Because you won't. You'll build a hypothetical or theoretically ideal organization that you think will work, but in practice will not work, and sabotage yourself from the get-go. You need to be realistic, setting rules and guidelines that everyone can easily follow. Then, bake in some element of challenge, so there is an embedded growth mindset. But don't overdo it. Make sure that you hold your team to a high standard, but not so high that people will fail to maintain that standard. Especially you. This will build very strong team cohesion and create mutual trust and respect within the team. But it must be consistent, and it must apply to everyone. It can get tricky, because not every division of the organization will have the same needs and structure. Certain divisions may need more flexibility, and others may need less. Certain personnel may desire some special circumstances here and there, while others do not. Put a lot of effort into this before you decide to implement anything, because once you choose your core rules and instructions, you don't want to change them and appear flippy-floppy and constantly alter things. That's a bad look as well. When done correctly, a set base of procedures, policies, rules, and guidelines that apply to everyone will set the foundation for team member accountability. This will result in a strong organization where employees bear mutual respect regardless of one's position. So again, think about this early in your organization's formation and implement rules thoughtfully so you do it once and do it right.

HOW TO AVOID DOUBLE STANDARDS:

- Make sure you have a written policy manual that outlines all the rules of the workplace.

- Make sure all employees read the policy manual and sign off on it.

- You must do the same, and you must work hard to follow the policies in place.

- If you don't want to follow a policy, you shouldn't make it a rule for others.

- Be sure you hold yourself and others close to you to the same standards as everyone else when you are in the workplace or conducting business.

- This will set a good example and make the workplace a fair and enjoyable place for employees.

Questions for Consideration:

Do you feel there are currently double standards in your organization? How is that hurting your company?

How would you and your team benefit by reducing double standards?

How will you implement this, and by when will you have this implemented?

MONEY WON'T MAKE YOU WEALTHY

Shifting gears a bit here, let's talk about what you're in it for. Why are you building this firm or organization? What is the bottom line here? Of course, we would all like to have money and be successful and be able to do whatever we please without any concern of financial limitations.

Money can make life so much easier. It can be seen as a tool to help you put efforts and resources into things you care about and support your passions. It can be a great thing. But you're not guaranteed to make a boatload. Most entrepreneurs and organizations never really make that much money. The billion-dollar success stories we hear about are few and far between, despite how often we hear about them. And in fact, many of these people who become mega-wealthy "overnight" find themselves isolated and alone because they are *perceived* as and *feel* so much different than most people.[8] It's called *sudden wealth syndrome.* It's been studied and verified, and sometimes the wealthiest people in our societies have some of the worst feelings of isolation and social distancing. Of course, this isn't always the case. Having a great deal of money can allow for people to build incredible networks and do great things. But in many cases, being incredibly wealthy is not what it's cracked up to be. The sad reality is that if you're in it for the money and only for the money, you'll be missing out on so much.

Money is really such a small part of what building a business or an organization is all about. Yes, you need the money; there's no way around that. You want it, of course. But it probably won't make you happy, and it definitely won't make you whole. It will give you a sense of satisfaction, but if that's all you care about, you'll find yourself glued to your net worth and probably incredibly distanced from many people. That's not wealth; that's having money, and they are two distinctly different things. No person can survive as an island for long, regardless of how much gold and silver is on that island. You don't have to look far to find that this is the truth. Do a quick search. Money does not equal happiness. Many times, money equals unhappiness—an ironic realization, no doubt. Now, I'm not suggesting you live in poverty or that giving all your money away is the key to happiness (even though some would argue it is), because it probably won't be. I'm just suggesting that if "making money" is the key driver behind your business or your organization, you will likely fail miserably. And if you succeed, you will probably be left wealthy and alone. Maybe fun, but not fulfilling.

Real wealth is having a strong sense of community, a network of people that look up to you and vice versa. It's having a sense of purpose and passion that you will continue to fight for regardless of the obstacles. It's having strength in your word and compassion for other people.

It's resiliency. It's good character. It's being surrounded by an energy of optimism and support so you know, without doubt, that other people have your back and they respect you and want you to succeed. It's the wisdom to understand that money comes and goes, but making a good impact on others will last far beyond your life. It's contributing to society and helping others out. It's sacrifice. It's virtue. It's the fact that people talk about you in a good way long after you have died. In a sense, it's a reflection of your value on Earth, but not by financial means.

Of course, you can have all these things and still become massively wealthy. In fact, having these traits and characteristics will make it far more likely that you will become massively wealthy because you will attract positive energy and good-natured people. You will be a magnet for success, without having to be greedy. In fact, your selflessness will make you financially rich, if you can believe that. One of my favorite quotes is from Bob Marley, and it goes, "Some people are so poor all they have is money."

As stated earlier in this book, the human existence is all about creating positive connections with other human beings. Add value for others and making money comes easy. So, as you sculpt your culture and the purpose of your startup or organization, be sure to set goals and virtues that are bigger than just making money. Make sure that you focus on elements that will bake in a sense of community, a sense of purpose, and a sense of pride. This will fuel your team more than simply making money; your growth will be real and not a silhouette. Once you can come from a foundation like this, the money will come. And when it does come, you will not focus solely on the money, but it will pour in. Because money is a by-product of your actions. It is something you are rewarded with for building a good organization.

Of course, there are companies out there that are designed just to make money, and there's nothing wrong with that. Being a middleman and reselling a product is simply buying someone else's product and selling it at a higher price. It's margin hunting, essentially. But you can do this in a way where money is not the focus. The focus is providing excellent service to others and delivering whatever awesome products you have, products that are aligned with a B Corp-type mentality made by companies that take care of their employees and consider the impact on all of their stakeholders. You can do this and be a middleman and create strong networks and work and act with integrity and respect. It really isn't that hard. In fact, it will make it so much easier for you to stay motivated. Because you're not just in it for the money, striving to make more and more. You have a bigger purpose. A bigger game. And that will help you trudge through the tough times much easier than just money hunting. Once you get to the other end of the swamp, with integrity, with a good team, and with positivity and a good purpose, there will be all the financial wealth you need. And chances are, you won't really care. You'll have enough for yourself, your team, and hopefully some extra to donate to your favorite charity or contribute to your favorite organization. And that is true wealth, and it's much greater than just having a good-looking bank account.

CREATE A CULTURE OF WEALTH IN YOUR WORKPLACE:

- Understand that wealth is about more than just money. Wealth can be about time, joy, your health, getting to do what you love, getting to learn more in a desired field, etc.

- Take time to understand what your employees want, and create a culture of wealth in your workplace. This could mean more time to socialize during the day, more freedom to express themselves, more opportunities for growth and learning, more flexible schedules, less overtime and an emphasis on life balance, a daycare at the workplace so they can see their kids, and more.

Questions for Consideration:

If you are honest with yourself, up to this point, has money been your main focus? If not, what things are you focusing on instead that make you feel wealthy?

Does your organization currently have a charity or cause it contributes to? If not, what would you like to contribute to in the future when you have the money?

How would doing so increase your passion for your work?

PART 4

PUTTING IT INTO ACTION

(UN)REALISTIC GOAL SETTING

OF COURSE, YOU'RE GOING TO WANT TO SET GOALS FOR YOUR organization. You'll need to. Otherwise, you're just shooting in the dark and will end up at some random destination. But setting goals can be tricky. If you're always setting goals that are unobtainable, then you will never hit them. If you are setting goals that are too easy to achieve, the goal-setting process is kind of pointless. It is best to set goals that are just challenging enough to be hard to hit, but that your team can reach (or almost reach), and not so challenging that they never hit them and are disappointed, leading to pessimism and cynicism. It's a fine line, no doubt.

Setting the proper difficulty for goals can be challenging. The goal must look a bit ridiculous at first glance, that it just cannot be reached given all the limitations you see in front of you. Yet under further scrutiny, you will see the possibilities line up. You will begin to see that, with a few tweaks here and a few tweaks there, along with some hard work and a bit of good fortune, it just might happen. An example of this could be sales goals. That's an obvious and usual target for startups. Or it could be in network connections. That's an obvious and usual target for organizations as well. Let's look at an example.

One founder, we'll call her Maria, did this successfully with increasing the company's connections on a social media platform. When she set the goal, her organization had a network of 10,000 connections, after two initial years of network building. She decided she wanted to push her team this year. She wanted them to think big. She set a goal to go from 10,000 connections to 100,000 connections in a year; a tenfold increase would be a large accomplishment. They pushed, hard. They used all their talent and resources and, in one year, made it to 85,000 connections. Sure, they fell short, but they made some incredible progress, learned a ton, and built their network base up massively. Maybe with a few tweaks here and there or a little bit of good fortune they would have hit that 100,000 target.

Now, say she had set the goal at 20,000 instead. That would still be a good target, doubling connections in a year, not bad by any means. But that would have likely gotten hit easily with some basic and general marketing tactics. Even just regular posting of good content would have likely achieved that. But it wouldn't have provided that "wow" factor and it wouldn't have pushed her team to try new things, utilize all their resources, and stretch their limits. It would have been growth, but fairly lazy and uninspiring growth.

Now, what if instead she set the goal at 1,000,000 total connections by the end of the year. A 100x increase. That is too big of a goal! It is more of a pipe dream that will never even come close to being reached. Her team could have tried everything and done everything imaginable and still likely only hit the 85,000 target with the more reasonable but yet slightly unrealistic 100,000 target. Shooting for 100,000 and hitting 85,000 as opposed to shooting for 1,000,000 and only hitting 85,000 has significantly different psychological impacts on a team. When you set a goal that is too large, where you set your team up for failure from the beginning, that does not make them want to work harder. It can reduce morale and leave them feeling that they can't trust you and your ability to accurately forecast results. They don't want to disappoint you, but it seems there is no way to please you when you try to push them that hard. Your leadership in their eyes will diminish, and it could be detrimental for the team.

I've experienced this firsthand when I initially partnered up with a buddy with his business. The company had less than $10,000 in annual sales at the time and we were talking to a potential investor about our desired growth, and the potential investor said, "Where do you see yourself in terms of gross annual sales in five years?" My business partner said, "Five billion a year in sales" (yes, BILLION) in five years. He thought we could go from $10,000 to $5,000,000,000 in annual sales in five years with very little capital with a manufacturing company that produced relatively inexpensive durable goods. That should have been my clue that my business partner did not know what he was doing. That his ability to gauge corporate growth was completely out of tune with reality. But I stuck with it, because I signed a contract and wanted to keep my word, and I knew he'd realize soon that was absurd, and he did. But this type of insanely unrealistic approach manifested itself in other areas of the company as time went on. Maybe not as dramatically, but it did occur and we fell short in many other areas of corporate forecasting, leading to a lot of distrust and discontent within the company. Can't say I didn't like the enthusiasm, though; maybe if he toned it down a notch it wouldn't have been so detrimental.

Goal setting, when done right, can be great for your team. It can help everyone be a part of the direction your organization wants to go. It can help you understand what your team is really made of and who is serious about massive growth and who is willing to go the extra mile. But as we've seen, it can be self-sabotaging if done improperly. If you don't take your limitations seriously, you're essentially wasting everyone's time with immature and highly unrealistic goals that will never be achieved. So, take it seriously and put time into it. As you achieve more and more stretch goals you will build an insane amount of confidence in your team. And as you keep knocking these goals down one by one, or at least getting very close to achieving them, you'll create momentum in the growth of your business. And momentum is highly valuable and useful for any organization, whether you have a startup or a mature company.

HOW TO SET A GOOD GOAL:

- The best way to set a goal is to talk with several people to decide a baseline for the goal that seems just out of reach for your team. This will ensure they stretch. Just make sure that the goal is not way too easy or way too hard.

- It is generally accepted that a good goal is a SMART goal, one that is:

  * Specific: targets a specific area for improvement

  * Measurable: can be measured quantifiably

  * Achievable: tells who can do it and how

  * (Un)realistic: can (un)realistically be achieved with the resources (un)available

  * Time-related: there's a specific target date or general time frame when the result(s) can be achieved

Questions for Consideration:

Have you set unrealistic goals in the past? How did that affect your company?

How will you make sure you are setting realistic goals that your team is on board with, while making them hard enough to make your team stretch?

By when will you have this implemented?

BUILDING MOMENTUM

PULLING A TRUCK WITH A ROPE IS INCREDIBLY CHALLENGING, but once you get it rolling, it picks up speed easier as you put in more effort. That's a lot like building a business or an organization. At first it seems so daunting and challenging. Everything takes so much work. It's overwhelming. The quote, "The journey of a thousand miles begins with a single step," comes to mind. You literally have to create the organization piece by piece, and there's so much work to do, it's incredible. Most businesses have to put in a tremendous amount of time, energy, and money before they even start seeing any revenue. It takes a leap of faith and incredible determination to get the wheels rolling. But once you start getting your product or service down, your core business principles established, and a handful of customers (repeat hopefully), then you can start seeing the fruits of your labor grow. It may happen slowly, but the progress will come if you just stick with it. Assuming you have some market pull and a desirable product or service, you just have to build that momentum.

To be clear on what momentum is, it's "the impetus and driving force gained by the development of a process or course of events."[9] It's the output of your input that should create more output as you put in more input. It can be thought of as a snowball. It starts small, but as it progresses, it slowly gets bigger and bigger, and before too long, it's massive! Well, a lot of the time that's how businesses and organizations grow. Another one of my favorite sayings goes something like this: "Every 'overnight success story' takes ten years to build." The point is, nothing happens overnight. It just doesn't. Go on, test the theory. Explore or examine any and every "overnight" success story you've heard of in business. I'd be willing to bet that you won't find one that didn't take at least five years to build before it became well-known and highly profitable. It rarely happens; it's an urban legend. Facebook, Oracle, Microsoft, Apple, LinkedIn, Uber, etc. all had founders who grinded for years, usually more like five to ten years, before they ever got on the map and were of interest to most people. Nothing happens that quickly when it comes to building businesses. There's a ton of sweat equity and hard work, with no guarantee of success, that goes into every single startup. However, once those initial years are grinded out, it can become so much easier. Once you have good customer churn, established supply chains, and an organization that is designed to scale growth, it can become relatively easy. Relatively. Not absolutely. It's never "easy." It just seems easier compared to the first few years. Usually.

So, you need to accept that realization. You need to come to terms with the fact that you will be grinding for years before you even become noticed by the market at large—at least most of the time. There are some instances where it can happen quicker, like a concept that is expedited through some crowdfunding site. But even then, you're on the hook to a bunch of micro-investors and haven't even developed a fully functional company yet. Just be forewarned; you will be grinding no matter what. And if you're not, there's a high likelihood that you'll fail. But if you keep grinding, something magical happens. You stop competing for customers. You stop grinding for pennies and start seeing dollars. Your customers begin to market your company for you, through word-of-mouth marketing—which, by the way, is one of the strongest forms of marketing. Sales pick up. You have all your vendors in line and your inputs secured. You have at least one method of marketing down and working for you, and the ball starts rolling. Little by little it gains more and more speed. You start listening to customers talk about how they heard about you. You start seeing online reviews show up for you—all good, hopefully. People start coming to you to carry your product or pitch your service. You'll feel a sense of relief, a realization that this is going to work. You have a viable business that people enjoy. It's almost as if you can take your hands off the wheel and relax. Almost, but not yet, because the grinding never stops—at least if you want to continue to grow your business or organization. There is always work to do. But now that you have an established organization it will be easier to manage in many respects. Now maybe you can hire an operations manager or some managerial assistance to take the load off of you. Now maybe you are seeing some profit and can relax a little bit knowing that you aren't going to go broke trying to grow this idea of yours. Now maybe you can relax and take some time off so you can rethink the next stages of your growth strategy. Now you can finally take a deep breath and be happy with what you have accomplished, because it is truly commendable. But it took time. It took determination. It took some serious resiliency, but you did it. And many people will respect you and look up to you for that. But it's a long game. Very long. If you look at some of the most well-known companies out there: BP, Coca-Cola, Unilever—they are decades and maybe even over a century old. Hardly overnight success stories.

It's in this initial momentum-building phase where the weak are weeded out. Entrepreneurs are pushed to the limit, and founders find out what they are made of. These are the critical years, in the beginning, when people begin to realize how incredibly hard it is to take an idea and turn it into a solvent and viable organization. It's a rude awakening for most founders. People see the success stories like Facebook and Uber and think that it's easy. Right? Take a good idea, add a few months of hard work, find a handful of investors to throw money at you, and there you go! You're making millions! And that's honestly how some people view it. Then reality hits, and then they get depressed, cynical, and start flailing. Then they fail. However, now you have this wisdom; you know what to expect. Just make sure that you're willing to put it all out on the line before you take the initial leap. Because failure sucks. It's inevitable for most, but it still sucks. So, prepare yourself mentally and get that ball rolling!

Another thing to mention that is incredibly valuable here is that once you create momentum and start seeing real progress, you must be careful not to lose it. It can happen in an instant. An economic downturn, a lawsuit due to an IP infringement, a competitor coming out of nowhere taking up your market share...there are many potential threats to your business, so stay aware. Monitor your surroundings and do your best to look for the things that could dampen your progress. It may take years to build up your business and gain highly valuable momentum, but it can take only a day to lose it all. I've experienced it firsthand.

Back when I was consulting in the cannabis industry I saw many beautiful and highly profitable gardens. But they do not appear overnight. They take a lot of work, investment, and dedication to get to a point where they run "flawlessly." It can take a year or two to get a grow operation "dialed in." You can imagine the stress. Invest thousands of dollars building a micro-climate to grow top-tier medicine in, only to have it underperform for months if not years. And then finally after much trial and error get it performing optimally. The money starts rolling in. People love the product and the books go from red to black in a matter of weeks. People are happy. Money virtually growing on trees. People buy nice things, take vacations, invest, whatever they want. But they also tend to get comfortable. They forget about all the dedication and attention to detail that was needed to get to this point. They start slacking. They may not notice that some type of pest or bug was introduced into the room. Maybe they're not paying attention to the climate and the humidity has been running high and mold or mildew is growing in places. Maybe the nutrients are off and they're not noticing that plants aren't producing like they should. Maybe the air filters are old and the neighborhood/complex is starting to smell (a violation in most "grow zones") and people aren't happy with that, or worse, potential thieves notice. That's when things start to go downhill. Because it only takes one or two issues to set off months of issues that need corrective action. I've seen perfectly good, optimal grow rooms crank out beautiful flowers for years only to be mismanaged due to over-comfort and then struggle for years. Getting into that groove is great, but once that happens, getting smug and comfortable can cost dearly.

So once you get to the point where you can take a step back and relax and your momentum is strong, don't get too comfortable. Don't take your eye off the ball and don't forget all the hard work and discipline that was needed to get here. Because this is the exact moment when surprises can come out of nowhere. Keep in mind that when things are going the best, you need to watch out for the worst. That way you don't get caught off guard and lose valuable momentum.

TIPS FOR CREATING MOMENTUM:

- Remember why you started the business, and use this passion to fuel you.

- Make good plans, set SMART goals, and start working toward them.

- Once you have a solid plan, commit to it until you reach your goal.

- If things aren't going as planned, analyze and see how you can change course.

- Be patient and celebrate the small successes along the way. The most persistent people, the ones who never give up in the face of adversity, are the ones most likely to succeed.

Questions for Consideration:

Have you started to gain momentum in your business? If not, or if you don't think it is happening quickly enough, what key factors are holding your business back?

What can you do about these things immediately and over the next year or so to start gaining more momentum?

What will you do in the meantime to keep yourself motivated?

By when will you have this implemented?

TO BE A HIGH-IMPACT TEAM, YOU MUST ACT LIKE ONE!

ALL OF THESE CONCEPTS AND IDEAS ARE ABSOLUTELY GREAT in theory. They're fun to learn about and help boost your knowledge base. Learning about different ways to build a business, how to solve problems, and how to lead people is essential for personal and organizational growth. But there is no value in learning if the lessons learned are not implemented. A person can learn everything and anything for years, but if they cannot put it into practice the knowledge is essentially useless. It is critical that you put these ideas and practices to work in the real world. You can't just learn stuff and expect that having the knowledge will get anything done for you. You must go from *concept* to *implementation*, and it's a lot of work. And that's one of the reasons that so many people fail after college. They think that because they went to school and learned a handful of things, they have real value in the world. They don't. Well, at least not until they put the knowledge to use in a practical and meaningful way. But until they do, it will just essentially sit in their brain and eventually fade away. Acting on the knowledge and leveraging it in a useful way is where you really begin to add value. And with the concepts in this book, you now know what it takes to be a high-impact team, but it's still just knowledge. Until you *act* like a high-impact team you will never *be* one. The power is in the action.

As you build your organization and continue to learn about so many useful tactics, like the ones you've read about in this book, it's critical that you find ways to implement them throughout your organization. For everyone. Do not attempt to implement all at once, as that would be quite overwhelming, and you still need to focus on the day-to-day elements of running your business. But eventually you're going to want to incorporate a good number of them, if not all, into your organization.

Which ones seem to be the most important for you? You will have to decide. There may be some that you feel you are already doing. There may be some that you don't want to focus on right now. And there may be some that are just too challenging for you and your team to truly attempt or master. Regardless, you must commit to some. At least have a list of a few that you really want to do, and always have one that is the focus of the team, that you are actively working on. Make it a priority to always be building your team, piece by piece, so that you are in action and putting these concepts into the real world.

Make a list of all the concepts you find valuable in this book, put them in order of the rank you deem most beneficial for you and your team, and then start chipping away. It's not going to come easily. Most of them will take days if not weeks, if not months, to be fully implemented and integrated into your team until you realize their full benefits. Some of them you will spend weeks to achieve and then realize, sometime later in the future, you somehow have completely fallen out of practice with them. In this case, it's usually best to revisit what went wrong and re-implement the practice. It happens a lot, and it's one of those things that most leadership coaches often don't mention: the fact that what they are teaching you will probably be forgotten and need to be refreshed. How many coaches who are charging four or five figures for their professional consulting would tell the hiring manager of a company that is paying for their services, "You know your team will probably forget all this in a month or two and you'll need to pay for a refresher"? Not many—sometimes because they don't want to lose business, and other times because they lack the integrity to admit that their work may take continuous commitment to remain effective. That's why it's up to you, the founder or critical manager, to make sure you are implementing these very valuable tools and also ensuring they stay implemented. You must also be wise enough to real-ize that some of them will fall out of practice, and it's up to you to get them back into focus. It's this level of consistency that will help you and your team catapult yourselves into a new and powerful future.

This is where it gets really difficult. This is where the rubber meets the road, so to speak. Everything we've talked about so far was all about "good ideas" essentially. Now you have to take "good ideas" and turn them into "good practices." You have to take the first steps. You have to hold yourself accountable to your word—to yourself and your promise to your team. On top of that, you have to keep your team accountable. You will make promises to each other and you will have to make sure they are fulfilled. This is where good leadership meets good business. It's one thing to create a successful organization in the first place, where you have a product or service that has market pull and is generating strong revenue. It's another thing to learn about and implement good leadership skills and characteristics. And it's an entirely different ball of wax to be able to build a successful organization, keep it running, and be able to keep learning and implementing good leadership practices at the same time.

Most of the time your daily business tasks will pull you away from thinking about leadership. Or worse, your "busy work" (hopefully *scheduled* work) may cause you to overlook proper leadership completely. It happens to the best of us. We get caught up in a project and become so self-absorbed in it that we fail to notice we are being bad leaders. On the contrary, we may get so focused on leadership that we stop thinking about the daily operational tasks we need to take care of. It's definitely a balance for sure, and it's one that you must work at incessantly. It's one that, as you continue to do it, will become easier. But again, we're back to the momentum element of it all. It starts slowly, and builds and builds on itself. The mountain of potential leadership concepts and tactics will whittle down over time as you practice them routinely, and they will be embedded into the core of your organization—which will be a magical thing. You will have a fully empowered team that is walking the talk and acting like a true high-impact organization.

HOW TO LEAD A HIGH-IMPACT TEAM:

- Now that you have learned the lessons in this book, it is time to apply them to your team. This could happen all at once or over time, but realize that you will have to do it more than once.

- Create a policy manual and training. One of the most important things you can do is put things in writing so people know what is expected. Train team leaders on the lessons in this book so they can carry them out in your business.

- Instate monthly meetings, and take an hour before work once a month to go over key things that need touching up. If you have a large group of employees and leaders for smaller groups, they will do the meetings for their teams. If you have a small group, you can do the meetings for the whole team.

- Any time issues start to flare up repeatedly, feel free to call a meeting or send out an email to remind employees of the way things are done in your workplace.

- Realize this is a constant process and slip-ups will occur. It is much easier to fix them quickly before they totally get out of hand and take more effort to correct.

Questions for Consideration:

What systems do you have in place or can you put in place to ensure that your team continues to implement the lessons you have learned in this book?

How will you know when you have let certain aspects slip and course correct?

By when will you have this implemented?

YOU SERVE YOUR EMPLOYEES; THEY DON'T SERVE YOU

THIS IS SO CRITICAL FOR FOUNDERS AND MANAGERS TO understand. It's a misnomer that since you're the founder, owner, or key manager of the company and it's your vision, the employees are all there to simply support you. That they are your helpers, your support staff, and yours to direct as you see fit. This is a horrible approach when you're trying to lead a team. It makes others feel like they are your subjects, your pawns, that their hopes and dreams somehow don't matter but yours do. In their reality, their dreams matter as well.

Everyone needs to have that feeling of hope and inspiration, the ability to express themselves and live the life they want to live—that one day their dream will come to fruition as well. Because when you have employees that come to work, follow your lead, help build your vision, and invest their precious time into your concept or idea, it can cause them to feel like they fall to the wayside, almost to the point where some people lose all their desire to dream.

As a founder, you must help build others up.

You must support them in their dreams and realize they're not there to supplant their dreams for yours. Show them that you appreciate them helping you build your dreams and you're there to help lift them up as well. This can be incredibly challenging for many founders because much of the time entrepreneurs are very focused on their own vision. I've seen founders who were coddled their entire life, growing up with the proverbial silver spoon in their mouth, constantly only focusing and caring about what's on their radar. Not only are they not paying any attention at all to the well-being of their team—not even going as far as to ask an employee how their weekend was—but they'll also sit and talk about themselves nonstop at work. They'll talk about how their weekend went, how their exercise routine is going, their relationship status, whatever. People will begin harboring resentment. People want to talk about their life, too, sometimes. They don't want to just go to work to make a paycheck, not be cared about, and listen to some self-absorbed business owner talk about themselves all day.

The reason why so many founders have trouble with this is simply because many may have huge egos. Face it, to believe in yourself enough to start a business, and market your product to the world, you have to have a massive amount of confidence. We talked about this in Lesson 20. The confidence levels for many founders are off the charts. Many times, so is their ego. And many times, they can be very selfish and think they are the center of the universe—at least the center of the company. This may be true, that they are the center of the company, but the organization cannot survive on just the founder alone. It takes a village. If you don't encourage your team members to feel like this is their village, too, and it's an environment that lifts them up, they're going to go build someone else's village elsewhere, or just try it on their own. There's no shortage of stories of competent employees that felt underappreciated by their boss who left and started their own thing. It happens a lot, usually with your best employees. They are the ones with the most intimate knowledge of your business. They have probably been there the longest (which has given them plenty of time to realize your selfishness), and they are the most skilled. But after so long they will leave you if they do not feel like they are appreciated and you are there to help them grow. It really is a quid pro quo. These employees will help you build your dream, but only if you help them build their dream. And it does take more than a paycheck a lot of the time. Here's another one of my favorite business quotes, this one from Richard Branson: "Train people well enough so they can leave, but treat them well enough so they don't want to." That's the point I'm trying to make. Realize that *you* serve your team. Always. I've seen so many employees start at new companies all excited and optimistic only to see them burned out and cynical years later. They weren't taken care of. They grinded for years for a measly paycheck while the founder went out and built the network traveling around the country, having fun, making far more money than everyone else, and owning the largest chunk of the company by far. They spent years grinding for someone else's business under the false premise that somehow they would be able to enjoy similar results, but received nothing. It sucks to see someone go from ecstatic to bitter in a few years, from excited to angry. I don't want to own a company full of resentful and hopeless employees, do you?

So how does a founder do this? How does someone focus on building their dream while supporting team members to build their dreams as well? A lot of hard work and focus. There's no way around it. You have to practice being present with your team to fully understand what they are trying to accomplish and what they desire. You have to listen to them genuinely to really hear what they are telling you. You have to be willing to be selfless and put their needs in front of yours at times. You have to allow for their self-expression and let them take the lead sometimes, trusting them in their judgments and their actions. And, you have to relax some control of your organization so others feel like you are an open and competent manager and leader, someone who really wants them to thrive and also have dreams.

Of course, it's not going to happen overnight. You must find a balance between pushing your dreams forward and staying cognizant of and being an assistant to their dreams.

Because, of course, if your organization fails, then there goes the team. It is a balance—a hard one at that. But like everything, the more you practice and the more you do it, the easier it becomes. Your teammates will see that you are being authentic with them and want them to have dreams in life that they are able to pursue and that you are willing to help them fulfill. And you know what? Something magical truly happens when your employees see this. Something usually gets triggered in them that wasn't there before. They realize they have a truly compassionate, thoughtful, caring, and selfless leader. And you know what else? Sometimes that's all people need to realize: that maybe, just maybe, their dream is helping you build your dream. That being a part of a team that has amazing values and practices, an amazing leadership team, a corporate vision and charter that is in line with their desires is all they truly want in their career path. After all, it's incredibly challenging to build a successful business from scratch. It takes a ton of hard work and time, and even then, most businesses will fail regardless. Some people don't even want to run their own company, and I don't blame them. Maybe all they want is to be a part of something bigger than them that has a sense of team and fulfillment. And if they have some ownership in your organization, maybe that's all they need. Maybe that's all they truly want? They have a piece of the pie, a great leader, and a good team that is focused on personal growth and development. Now they don't have to look any further. Now maybe, just maybe, your dream has become their dream too.

HOW TO BECOME A SERVANT LEADER:

- Take a genuine interest in your people and learn their strengths and weaknesses.

- Determine if you have a team that has lower knowledge and needs more guidance from you or a team that has high knowledge and needs little guidance from you. Treat your team accordingly for best results.

- Become comfortable with letting them take charge and do things their way as long as they reach predetermined targets. This will take the pressure off of you and allow people to harness the passion for their work, making you all more productive in the end.

- Learn to help your people grow and reach their goals in your business, so they will want to keep working there.

Questions for Consideration:

Take an honest look at the way you currently run your business. Is it more about fulfilling your dreams or helping your team fulfill theirs?

What steps can you start taking today to ensure that your team feels like your workplace is helping them fulfill their dreams and goals?

By when will you have this implemented?

YOUR AGE DOESN'T MATTER

THIS CAN BE A CONTENTIOUS TOPIC. IT IS ONE THAT PEOPLE can develop all types of arguments for and against. It's the belief that your age doesn't matter, that you have capabilities and opportunities at any and all stages of your adult life. Of course, if you're eighteen years old, you'll lack relative wisdom but likely make up for it with energy and youthful optimism. And if you're sixty-eight years old, you'll possibly lack energy but make up for it with incredible wisdom and experience.

With today's interconnected virtual world, anything is possible if you're willing to learn what tools you need to accomplish your vision. There's a common misnomer that the only truly successful entrepreneurs are twenty-to-thirty-something Silicon Valley tech geniuses that create new and exciting software and apps. That couldn't be further from the truth.

In fact, recent studies show that the average age to become an entrepreneur is in your mid-forties.[10] Yup, "middle-aged" people, those with years of experience and plenty of energy and insight, are known to be some of the most successful founders out there. On top of that, there is a massive push with people in "un-retirement," those sixty-five years or older. They are technically retired but are either starting their own organization or working well into their eighties in groups and organizations just for the fun of it and to maintain some mental acuity. You don't need to be a twenty-or-thirty-year-old tech genius to be an entrepreneur or start an organization. You just don't.

It can seem incredibly daunting at any age, however. It doesn't matter how old you are; starting an organization is a lot of work. But getting past the fact that you're "too young" or "too old" is a major psychological achievement. Many times, humans tend to create obstacles because we know that what we want to undertake is going to be very challenging and we might fail (revisit Lesson 13 if you still feel this way), so we make excuses not to try. But your age isn't one of them. The truth is it's all about your mindset. You must believe in yourself regardless of your age. If you choose to, you can find an excuse no matter how old you are. If you're twenty years old you could easily say, "I'm too young and inexperienced." If you're forty you could say, "I can't take this risk at this age. I have to think about retirement." If you're sixty you could say, "I'm too old to start an organization." You see, it doesn't matter because if you want to find an excuse you surely will. It's best to realize that no matter how old you are, it's the right time to start. "I'll do it later" is one of the worst things you could say to yourself. "I missed my window" is another horrible thing to tell yourself. The bottom line is that today is the day to begin. There is no tomorrow, the past is long gone, and no matter how old you are you just have to take the leap. It's daunting for everyone. There are challenges galore, and you are not guaranteed anything. But the desire to do your own thing and take the leap of being a founder is in you for a reason. You're not cut out for the traditional office job, or whatever traditional job may be out there waiting for you. You're reading this because you're looking for inspiration and guidance, some type of nudge or encouragement. But at the end of the day, it all comes down to you taking the leap. Maybe you're a twenty-year-old who just can't seem to hold a job and doesn't really do well with authority, so you have to create something on your own. Maybe you're a forty-year-old who is looking at retirement, don't feel set for it, realize your current job is not going to get you prepared, and you just need to give your ambitions a chance. And maybe you're that sixty-year-old who has just recently retired, and you are already bored and need some stimulation and networking, and have an idea for an organization you've been thinking about for years. Whichever you are, it doesn't matter—your age, your sexual orientation, your race, your family background, your religious beliefs, nothing. None of that matters. The only thing that matters is that you find a passion and learn how to turn it into a useful product or service and you give it everything you have. Again, yes, you might fail. But if you take the wisdom in this book and apply it in practice, your odds of success will be much higher than if you just went out on a limb and "shot from the hip," so to speak.

Another one of my favorite quotes is from Jeff Bezos, founder of Amazon.com. Back before Jeff started Amazon.com, he had a relatively nice job as a senior vice president at a hedge fund. He could have kept his comfortable job and lived a very great life, but he saw massive opportunity in this new "internet commerce." Mind you, this was back in 1993, and e-commerce was just catching on. He really wanted to capitalize on this new technology that he was certain was going to be a big deal soon enough. He had a decision to make. Go out on a limb and start an e-commerce business or play it safe and keep the hedge fund job. Obviously, he took the leap and started Amazon.com. Years down the road someone asked him something like, and I'm paraphrasing, "Jeff, Amazon was such a gamble. You had a great life. Why did you take the risk of entrepreneurship when you were doing so well?" Bezos replied, "I knew that if I failed, I wouldn't regret that, but I knew that the one thing that I might regret is not trying." That's not an uncommon sentiment for people when they get into their later years. It's not usually about what you did that was regretful; it is about what you didn't do. If you're on the fence still, even after making it all the way through this book, and still looking for an excuse not to take the leap, it's not there anymore. Whatever age you are, take the positive from it and apply it to your dreams, your passions. "Too young," use that energy to its fullest. "Too old," take some of that wisdom and experience and teach the younger generations. We need it now more than ever. We need to put aside agism and create value for each other at any and all stages of life. There's so much to learn from each other, and your age is no longer a hindrance; it's a blessing, regardless of how many spins around the sun you've taken.

BE A GOOD LEADER REGARDLESS OF YOUR AGE:

- **Learn to listen.** We have covered listening many times in the book, and you can see by now there are several different ways a good leader uses listening to get to know his employees so he can utilize them to their fullest.

- **Innovate.** A good leader knows how to steer around obstacles. If you want to keep your business afloat, you may have to remake it several times, or at the very least tweak it, so it can continue to be successful.

- **Have heart.** Good leaders have passion for what they do that spills over to their team.

- **Have ideals.** A reason bigger than your business will make you and your team work harder toward a common goal.

- **Don't be afraid to roll up your sleeves and get to work.** Lead by example. Showing others that you work as hard as they do is a great way to motivate them.

Questions for Consideration:

If you currently have doubt around your age, what are some ways you can eliminate it? What strengths do you feel you have because of your age?

Are there other factors you think cause people to discriminate against you as a business founder? If so, how can you start to overcome those?

By when will you have this implemented?

YOU MUST BELIEVE IN YOURSELF AND YOUR TEAM

THE IDEA FOR THIS LESSON CAME LATE FOR ME. I HAD THE first twenty-nine lessons completed and started to look at proofreaders and editors to help me finalize the book. But then a lot of doubt started to cast over me. The whole "imposter syndrome" started to kick in. I'm no multimillionaire coach. I don't have oceanfront houses and no one has invited me to be a guest on their TV show. Sure, I've helped create some successful businesses, but I'm not a bigwig venture capitalist or anything like that. Yeah, I have a relatively thorough and expansive education, but I'm not a doctor. There are no buildings at my university named after me. And then I started really digging into these thoughts. I thought to myself, "Well, these things have not happened yet." I have yet to become a successful millionaire coach or consultant. I have yet to be asked to do a TV interview and go live across the country. I have yet to do a lot of these things. But does that mean that I won't accomplish these things? Does that mean I'm not worthy or capable of accomplishments like this? Only if I believe these thoughts to be true. If the thoughts of self-doubt perpetuate, then it's unlikely I will ever achieve anything to the contrary. But if I truly believe that I will overcome these perceived shortcomings, then the possibilities open up. This may sound very similar to the neuroplasticity and self-talk lesson, but it runs a bit deeper. It's the core belief in yourself that you are limitless and can achieve anything you truly set your mind to. Yes, you need positive affirmation and healthy self-talk, but you also have to believe it to be true. Without the belief in yourself you'll never truly dedicate yourself to your dreams. It will continue to feel like you're faking it, and that will hold you back.

It can be easier to have this belief in yourself when you're cruising, doing well in life (think back to the lesson on momentum; your positive thoughts and belief in yourself can develop momentum too). But what about when things crater around you? What about when times are tough? How about after you've lost a job, or had health issues? Maybe you just failed at numerous startups and can't find any glimmer of hope, or you just lost a bunch of cash on a bad business investment or risky gamble. It's in these times of chaos and uncertainty that you really must find faith in yourself. After all, it's possible that some of the best times to create a new path, whether it be a business, a hobby, or a life focus, are during times of turmoil. It's during these times that we must look deep within ourselves to see what we're made of.

Take the time to do some inner work. Look at what you have been trying and what has been working and what hasn't been. Ditch the hobbies, habits, thoughts, and actions that have failed you and your team, and maximize the ones that have. What has been in the dark for you now needs to be brought into the light. If your organization has been focusing on making widget X but sales haven't been robust enough, maybe try out that widget Z idea that you've been contemplating for so long. If your company focuses on consulting in the travel industry and now the industry is down 95 percent year-over-year, with a long road to recovery, maybe try a different angle. But the most important thing is that you must believe in yourself and your team. You absolutely must keep the faith and hope alive. You must trust that this is all a part of the journey, that these are lessons and experiences that will help you become a better you and build a better team. There's no way around it. You're a winner, and you're reading this book because something inside you knows this. You just have to fervently believe it.

There are no guarantees in life, and believing you're a winner and that you're going to be successful isn't going to automatically make it happen. But the odds of it happening if you think you're a loser are close to zero. So, make the choice to be positive. That's the base of your platform—self-love, optimism, compassion, faith, and fight. And if you're reading this and this hasn't been an issue for you (some people have always been optimistic and believed in themselves), that's awesome. Kudos to you and keep it up. But if you haven't always been this way, if you've been cynical, pessimistic, and lacked hope and don't know where to turn...don't give up, don't give in. Keep grinding and pushing forward. Your team, your business, and you are relying on it.

This all brings me back to J. K. Rowling's story (the creator of the Harry Potter book series). Before she hit it big, she was in a very rough spot. She was recently divorced, had a child that she could barely take care of financially, was fighting depression, and had contemplated suicide.[11] She was in a very, very bad place in her life. The idea for Harry Potter had already been formulated in her mind, but the feedback she was getting from publishers wasn't the most optimistic. She was essentially told, "Don't quit your day job." It looked bleak for her. Everything in her life was falling apart. Yet, she pushed on and wrote her first Harry Potter book, *Harry Potter and the Sorcerer's Stone*, in 1995 using an old manual typewriter. The book slowly gained traction. There was enough positive feedback for her to get a small grant and continue writing. She wrote another Harry Potter book, and another, and another. Eventually, the first book was made into a movie, then another, then another. The rest is history.

Now, do we need to or necessarily desire to become that wealthy and famous? Do we want to build massive multi-billion-dollar enterprises? Some of us do, but most of us likely don't. Most of us just want to live comfortably and be challenged just enough and enjoy maybe raising a family without worrying about how we're going to afford our lifestyles. Personally, I don't aspire to become a billionaire. I would be comfortable making a low six-figure salary (I wouldn't scoff at more, of course) and having enough freedom and flexibility of my time to travel the world, surf, go on adventures, take photos of amazing locations and eat wonderful food, help build businesses, and work with amazing people. We all have our ideal life. That's mine, so what is yours? Go ahead and think about it for a minute. Envision it. Enjoy the possibility of it. Regardless of what it is, it's quite likely obtainable. Then, believe that you can make it happen. When times are good, when times are bad, when we are up, and when we are down, it all comes back to you and your fight. Don't ever forget it. You've got this. You are worthy and so is your organization, your team, your family, all of it. Nothing is stopping you but you. Now, let's go crush it...

Fortune favors the bold!

ABOUT THE AUTHOR

LIKE MOST PEOPLE, I DIDN'T GROW UP WITH A SILVER SPOON in my mouth. I haven't given lectures at prestigious universities or rubbed elbows with dignitaries. I grew up in a standard middle-class family in Orange County, California. Yes, I feel fortunate to have been born in Fountain Valley, California, and grow up in Huntington Beach, California. It's such a beautiful and opportunistic place. But it wasn't all fun and games.

I was the product of both my parents' second marriages, my mother bringing in three children from her first marriage and my father bringing in one child from his first marriage. We almost had the whole *Brady Bunch* thing going on, sans one more child and a maid. But money was tight and always a point of tension. My older brothers weren't necessarily the most well-behaved, and there were constant family squabbles. But I was smart, athletic, genuine, and gifted, and had a good path in front of me.

At ten years old I was in all the accelerated courses in school (GATE, I believe they were called, for gifted and talented education) and a straight-A student. I was ranked in the top ten of athletes for my age group for youth soccer in AYSO region 117 (a highly competitive and talented region nationally for soccer) and was dating my "first love" (at ten years old we were already talking about getting married and raising a family—such innocence). But it all fell apart at twelve when the divorce happened.

My world unraveled.

The family blew apart. My father went a new way, found a new wife, and started a new family within a year or so. My mother stayed in the area for a while, while my brothers all went their own ways. I started doing drugs and alcohol. I went from a top-tier student, top-ranked athlete, and positive and grounded adolescent to a Grateful Dead–listening, binge-drinking, psychedelic-eating young teenager. By the time I made it to high school I was smoking weed nonstop, getting blackout drunk, and going to school on "magic mushrooms." I had lost all faith. At fifteen I was sure I'd be dead by eighteen. I was the by-product of a failed marriage. There was no love left. My world imploded, my family left me, and all I had left were my friends and my drugs. It all happened within two years.

My father pulled me out of public high school in Fountain Valley after freshman year. He saw the road I was going down and wouldn't allow it. He put me into a private Christian high school up in Cerritos, California. I fought it, but it worked, and I eventually graduated in 1999. I immediately moved out of Southern California. I had $500 I'd borrowed from a friend and an old 1984 Chevy Blazer that barely ran. That was it. I had no backup plan. No safety net. But I went to the mountains to snowboard (my newfound passion) regardless. I wanted to escape, and the mountains gave me everything I was looking for. First it was Mammoth Mountain, California, for a winter. Then eventually I found my way to Lake Tahoe, California, where I lived for seventeen years.

But I was still me when I left So Cal. Moving from the beach to the mountains didn't change me at all. I was still on drugs and a party animal. At nineteen I thought for sure I would not live to see twenty-one. At twenty-one I thought for sure I'd never live to see twenty-five. I didn't have much hope, nor vision; I was cynical and lost. Snowboarding was my love, and my drugs and friends were my support groups. That was me.

One morning when I was twenty-four years old, I woke up after a night of partying with friends. I felt horrible. My heart was beating out of my chest. I needed to get healthy. I decided to go for a morning run (a pathetic attempt at reversing twelve hours of nonstop partying). It was during this run that I had my first, and so far only, epiphany.

While I was "cooling down" from my short and strenuous jog, I had a thought: "What if I *do* live to see twenty-five? In fact, what if I do live to see thirty years old, and then maybe forty, and then fifty, or longer? If I stay on this path, I'll be a loser forever. I'll be like my friend's parents who are in their forties and sit around and drink beer with their high school kid's friends and talk about the 'good old days.' That's going to be me." At that point, I made a choice. I wouldn't turn into that "low-life." I wouldn't let all my parents had worked for, what they tried to and wanted to accomplish for me, go to waste. I had it in me. I was a superstar. I was incredibly smart, athletic, genuine, and gifted, like most all of us. No, I wasn't going to give up anymore. I was going to make something of myself.

I almost immediately moved out of the six-person party house I was living in. I got my own place and started grinding. After a year, I put myself back into college. (I tried community college at nineteen; I lasted all of three months.) I studied what I loved: philosophy, psychology, and business. I enjoyed it, and it was engaging and challenging for me, so I stuck with it. Fast-forward twelve or so years and I had multiple college degrees: associate's degrees in liberal arts and accounting, bachelor's degrees in economics and international business, and an MBA with a focus in entrepreneurship. I helped a buddy build a business out of his house that turned into a globally known brand with a large team and big warehouse. I took multiple leadership and business courses and, after fighting off my travel anxiety for half a decade, traveled to Spain, Mexico, Italy, Costa Rica, Thailand, Indonesia, and New Zealand. I married a beautiful and complete woman; we eloped and got married in Italy. I had accomplished a lot, and it was all because I believed in myself.

Why do I share this with you? I'm not tooting my own horn or attempting to brag. I do it because I want to connect. I want to show that I'm a person who has had a rough road, too. It wasn't all fun and games. My family didn't come from wealth, and we didn't live lavish lifestyles. And yours probably didn't either. Even if you did, you still likely had issues, still had problems, doubts, and concerns. You may still have portions of your past holding you back, keeping you stuck and unable to move forward. And that brings me to the second reason I'm sharing this: so I can reconcile with my past. I let the divorce and my subsequent thoughts of myself (the "I'm not loved," the "I'm worthless," and the "I won't live another five years" thoughts that I developed as a kid) create a new me—a worse me. I let that one incident drastically alter my perception of myself, of my family, of my faith, and of my world. It changed me beyond recognition.

Now, I'm closing the chapter on those thoughts, bringing myself back to the me before the divorce. And by stating what I experienced—so bluntly, so boldly, so raw, to essentially strangers—I'm releasing that past. I'm owning it and exercising it. I can now clearly see where things took such a nasty turn, and I'm shutting the door on it all so I can create a better me. The authentic me. The superstar me—the person worthy of love and affection. The person that wasn't constantly self-destructing with drugs and alcohol. The person who had a positive outlook on life and could become *anything*. But it has taken me over twenty-five years and a lot of work to get here. The road to completion hasn't been easy, it rarely is, and it never ends.

Now here I am, making changes and choices to help heal myself and others, and I'm still holding myself back. I still let things from the past get to me, because the negativity and self-doubt doesn't just disappear. We are constantly bombarded with doubt and uncertainty, and maybe not even from ourselves, but from others. In recent years I've had business partners say, "You're not as good as you think you are" or "You're a small person." If I allow myself to take their subjective opinion as truth, they will be correct. But I will not, and you should not. I'm much better than I or they think I am; I am infinitely capable. I am a big person, ready and willing to make a positive impact for countless people. I am not slowing down or turning back; I am only charging forward. Because I know, as should you, that we're only a conversation, a chance meeting with a stranger, a single product idea, a great read (wink), or a ring of the phone away from our lives being altered forever.

Whether it's a new business concept, a new job, a new diet, or a new whatever, one day can change the path of your life forever. And if you believe that you are destined for greatness, that you are worthy of living your authentic life, it is very possible that you will achieve it all. But to move forward in a new and promising light, we must shed our negative and destructive past. Joseph Schumpeter, the Austrian political economist, calls it "creative destruction." This is the practice of destroying something to create space for something new and better to grow. It's re-creation. When we re-create, we are destroying old cells, weaker cells, and building new, stronger ones. And we must continually do it. If we re-create negatively, that's what we'll get as an outcome, negative results. If we re-create positively, then we become more positive.

It's said that almost every cell in our bodies is regenerated over time.[12] Very few cells in our bodies are the same cell from ten years ago. They have most all died and been reproduced. Give it a good, long think. Think about your diet, your exercise habits, your self-talk. Do they reflect the person you are now? More than likely. I know mine do. Now choose to re-create yourself as a new, better, stronger, more compassionate and giving person. Put good thoughts, good food, and good actions into your being and let yourself build with positivity and optimism and see where it gets you. But you must take action. You must eliminate the noise. Cut out all the distractions. Eliminate social media unless you're promoting your passion. Turn off your TV and get rid of the toxic and destructive mainstream media. Stop your bad habits that make you feel unhealthy and hold you back. Remember, the mind and body are intertwined. Eating healthy helps you think healthy, and thinking healthy can motivate you to be healthier.[13] Create a laser focus on something that will bring you massive happiness, not just mere distractions and mindless entertainment. It will not be easy, it will take work, but you will look back on your life with a sense of honor and purpose, and it will be worth every struggle, every pain, and every setback you ever had. In the end, you will be able to say that you conquered your fears and demons and left this world a far better place than when you entered it. And that, my friends, is worth a whole lot more than money.

ENDNOTES

1 **Global attention span shortening:** Technical University of Denmark, "Abundance of Information Narrows Our Collective Attention Span," *Nature Communications*, April 15, 2019, https://www.eurekalert.org/news-releases/490177.

2 **Humans have bad memories:** Rachel Barclay, "Your Memory Is Unreliable, and Science Could Make It More So," HealthLine, September 13, 2013, https://www.healthline.com/health-news/mental-memory-is-unreliable-and-it-could-be-worse-091313.

3 **God spoke into existence:** Psalm 33:9, "For he spoke, and it came into being; he commanded, and it came into existence," *The Christian Standard Bible*, Copyright 2017 by Holman Bible Publishers.

4 **The power of self-talk:** Susan York Morris, "What Are the Benefits of Self-Talk?," HealthLine, updated December 19, 2016, https://www.healthline.com/health/mental-health/self-talk.

5 **Three weeks to change your brain:** Phillippa Lally et al., "How are habits formed: Modelling habit formation in the real world," *European Journal of Social Psychology* 40, no. 6 (July 16, 2009): 998–1009, https://onlinelibrary.wiley.com/doi/abs/10.1002/ejsp.674.

6 **Creating new neural pathways:** Julie Hani, "The Neuroscience of Behavior Change," Startup+Health, August 8, 2017, https://healthtransformer.co/the-neuroscience-of-behavior-change-bcb567fa83c1.

7 **Isolation a cause of depression:** Julianne Holt-Lunstad, "The Potential Public Health Relevance of Social Isolation and Loneliness: Prevalence, Epidemiology, and Risk Factors," *Public Policy & Aging Report* 27, no. 4 (January 2, 2018): 127–30, https://academic.oup.com/ppar/article/27/4/127/4782506.

8 **Wealthy people and loneliness:** Alina Dizik, "Loneliness Often Follows Sudden Wealth," BBC, October 17, 2016, https://www.bbc.com/worklife/article/20161014-loneliness-often-follows-sudden-wealth.

9 **Definition of "momentum":** Encyclopedia.com, s.v. "Momentum," updated May 23, 2018, https://www.encyclopedia.com/science-and-technology/physics/physics/momentum.

10 **Average age to become entrepreneur:** Nidhi Singh, "What Is the Ideal Age to Be An Entrepreneur?," Entrepreneur, August 10, 2018, https://www.entrepreneur.com/article/318298.

11 **J. K. Rowling:** Wikipedia, s.v. "J. K. Rowling," last modified February 2, 2022, 16:54, https://en.wikipedia.org/wiki/J._K._Rowling.

12 **Cellular regeneration:** "How Quickly Do Different Cells in the Body Replace Themselves?," Cell Biology By the Numbers, accessed October 21, 2021, http://book.bionumbers.org/how-quickly-do-different-cells-in-the-body-replace-themselves/.

13 **Eating healthy helps you think healthy:** David Lipps, "How the Food We Eat Affects Our Brains and Bodies," Kaiser Permanente, October 17, 2019, https://about.kaiserpermanente.org/total-health/food-for-health/food-for-thought/how-the-food-we-eat-affects-our-brains-and-bodies.

CPSIA information can be obtained
at www.ICGtesting.com
Printed in the USA
JSHW041441190422
24962JS00001B/1